# THE VITAL FEW
# NATURAL LAWS

## Powering the 80/20 Methodology in Business

PEDRO FERRO

# DEDICATION

To my Family.

# CONTENTS

# INTRODUCTION

*The purpose of a business is to create a customer.*

*— Peter Drucker*

The notion that businesses perform at their best when managers embrace practices that emanate from natural laws has been growing on me throughout my entire professional life. With enough experience, you come to realize that the essence of management revolves around making choices and navigating through a sea of complexity and ambiguity. It's one challenge after another, and it helps enormously to have your own boat to sail through the madness with relative calm: A personal set of tools and beliefs that you hold true in your most personal self and that you can always come back to whenever you have doubts. A set of principles that works every time and everywhere and that, even if it is very basic, can be stretched to reach into the most complex management issues.

One of these very basic beliefs is the Pareto principle, or the natural law of the vital few and the trivial many. Pareto[i] and later Juran[ii] were good and reliable friends during my engineering days. I've always resorted to this principle, which is also called the 80/20 rule, to prioritize and to understand imbalances at work. It helps me decide which problems to attack first and how to address product quality and service issues. It didn't take me long to figure out that the 80/20 rule is extremely applicable in business. The principle and the belief in this natural law came in handy as the companies I've worked for applied well-known improvement methodologies such as lean and six sigma across different operations. I saw visible results from these practices, but I always felt there was something missing in relation to

1

transforming the businesses to reach new levels of performance, sustain profitability, and creating what Warren Buffett calls a "wide and deep economic moat."

As your career evolves into more senior and significant leadership roles, you will come to understand the value of simplicity and the impact that unmanaged complexity has on the bottom line. You will realize that, by trying to do too much and being comprehensive, you are in reality creating complexity for yourself and for others. You will come to understand that managers must develop the ability to become selective by using what I call asymmetric decision-making to identify, choose and apply the vital few inputs that will produce the best results with the least effort. Because simplicity is highly connected to the 80/20 rule, or the law of imbalances, it helps us recognize that managers do not have the luxury or resources available to cover all of the bases. After a few years as a manager, I already knew that efforts and decisions did not have equal value in business, but as I've gained experience, I've learned that simplification is one of the most important disciplines that needs to be constantly applied by managers.

Sooner or later, you will be confronted with the challenge of turning around or significantly improving a business, with the goal of transforming it into an enterprise capable of growing and creating lasting value. This task came to me when I was made an officer at Cummins. I began worrying about developing an embryonic division, based on providing information technology services to customers. I realized then the importance of innovation to change a company for good, taking it to a new and unexpected level of performance. I already knew that product invention and patents were essential, but my thinking was limited in scope. And I also had misconceptions about how to foster and drive innovation into the business. As we started to reshape the future of the company with a new strategy, I discovered the power and the benefits of systematic and multidimensional innovation that goes beyond product invention and into the business model. I understood that leaders must create conditions and instill thinking that will promote innovation in deliberate ways rather than relying on great ideas or strokes of genius alone. Innovation and evolution became synonymous to me and entered my personal toolbox forever.

Then came Dell Computer Corporation during the heyday of the late 90s. I was faced with the challenge of marketing rapidly commoditizing computers to a changing customer base, using sales tools that I had only read about. It was the "Dell Direct Model" or Dell's way of selling straight to end users through the Internet. The sharpness and extreme focus at very well-defined customer segments (e.g., students at K–12 and higher education, employees with federal, state and local governments) through smaller, independent business units opened my eyes to the fact that an existing customer base can offer almost unlimited growth opportunity. The illusion that a market segment is rigidly structured is just that, an illusion. Dell showed me that it's always possible to look deeper into an existing customer-base segment and find new similarities between customer sub-groups and fresh needs to fulfill, generating incremental sales and profits.

After Dell, my personal toolbox had four principles that I could launch to improve businesses and to deal with management challenges:

- Business life is imbalanced, and there are only a small number of vital inputs that produce the majority of the outputs. The rest are the trivial many that create noise and can drag you down.

- Simplification is a necessity. Left on its own, a business gets complex over time, filling up with activities and costs that are not necessarily aligned with the mission of taking care of customers and innovating.

- Markets and customer segments are not monolithic. You can always find additional value within your existing market if you understand customer's self-similarities and specialize your value proposition to deliver to either spoken or unspoken needs.

- Innovation, in the broader sense of the word, is the only way to create new levels of performance in terms of growth, margin, and value. Everything else is short-term incremental work.

Dell was constantly "creating" new market segments within existing segments to deliver new products and services, such as computer and storage configurations, printing options, support services, and so on. The list of products and services invented to cater to segments of the ever-expanding customer base was endless. Dell was fulfilling what Peter Drucker declared in his book The Practice of Management[iii]: "Because the purpose of business is to create a customer, the business enterprise has two — and only two — basic functions: marketing and innovation. Marketing and innovation produce results; all the rest are costs. Marketing is the distinguishing, unique function of the business."

Dell understood its customer segments and supply chains to be extensions of its core business. It gave customers the ability to create personalized websites with their own exclusive catalog of Dell's products and prices. Corporate customers were given tools to manage purchases made directly by their employees in multiple locations, so prices and specs were consistent across the enterprise. Dell imparted to me the importance of market-segment-focused business units (BUs). Their customer focus and ability to innovate were impressive. Dell also taught me the power of segmentation and showed me the fractal nature of the markets. Later, when I moved on to the Marmon Group, I fully realized the importance of combining market segmentation a la Dell with the sharp focus and effectiveness of independent BUs a la 80/20.

Many outstanding companies combine these four natural laws into their own business systems. Besides Cummins and Dell, I can name a few, such as GE, Google, Illinois Tool Works (ITW), Marmon-Berkshire Hathaway, and Danaher, as prime examples. Almost all business improvement methodologies used by these and many other companies today contain these principles in one form or another, for example, six sigma (DMAIC), lean, Deming Cycle (PDCA), Business Process Reengineering (BPR), Toyota Production System (TPS), and others.

When you look closer at other success stories similar to those of Cummins and Dell, you realize what Drucker was saying: the heart of every successful business is located right at the intersection of customers and products or services, which are the vehicles to deliver innovation to markets. Without a constant effort to optimize and evolve these fundamental company assets, it's difficult to sustain growth and profitability for a long period of time.

This brings us to the basic management challenge of perfecting the alignment between people, resources, and value adding activities, including making products available and creating and retaining customers. It's imperative to understand whether these activities are focused on what is most important for the business. But knowing how it all adds value and aligns with the mission is not a trivial question to answer. Most of the time, managers use their best judgment and intuition to decide how to allocate or reallocate resources. But factual data and critical thinking also need to be applied to determine where the center of gravity is in relation to the company's vital few inputs.

If you had to serve only one customer with one product, your business would be a lot simpler and easier to manage. In the real world, companies are dealing with a multitude of customers and a large number of product lines. They are also dealing with complexity and artificiality. But in every case, there are a smaller number of customers and products responsible for the bulk of revenues and profits. Furthermore, in almost every case, you can find poorly allocated capital and unengaged people serving the least important aspects of the business, due to complexity-driven mission myopia. So how do you ensure that your best, most valuable resources are being applied to the customers, products, services, and processes responsible for the bulk of the profits?

We go back to natural causes and effects. At the root of the problem lies the unfailing ability that human beings have to complicate things for themselves and for others. In today's very complex business world, managers forget there is a real need to simplify and keep unnecessary complexity from adding cost and muddying up the waters. Managers don't always draw the line between too much complexity and just the right amount of structure and controls.

One of the problems with complexity is that, if not managed, it creeps in over time along with revenue growth. Very few companies proactively manage the amount of clutter and complexity in the business. You will find a world of metrics out there, but few are related to measuring and reducing complexity. I will expand on ways to manage and reduce complexity later on, but for now it suffices to know that it grows with the business and drives costs up without adding proportional value. People full of good intentions unknowingly create complexity every day.

Conventional metrics from accounting and reporting systems do not help either. Instead they create information that is not very useful for that purpose. Most manufacturing-cost accounting systems, for example, adequately arrive at the cost of goods sold for fiscal and regulatory purposes, but they rarely help managers understand the real contribution margins in real-time. They tend to spread or allocate fixed costs and overhead over all production orders based on arbitrary criteria such as labor hours. This is jokingly referred to as the "peanut butter approach," since every product gets a dose of overhead, regardless of how much complexity goes into its production. Instead of knowing exactly what it costs to make a widget, managers get an approximation derived from a complicated labor and cost allocation methodology. Not to mention the enormous amounts of hours and resources spent to update standards for these expensive IT systems to further allocate production costs. Business IT systems continue to be sold every day on the premise of providing useful management information, but very few deliver on the promise of reducing complexity.

Another issue is the proliferation of products and part numbers, which is one of the biggest drivers of complexity and cost to a business. Well-intentioned people, trying to serve customers at all costs, sneak in more part numbers and product items every day. In some markets, product line breadth and complexity management is what companies do. Companies like Amazon, for example, profit from servicing the long tail of complexity. They specialize in servicing the low volume products at a premium price. There is nothing wrong with this model, as long as the business is being adequately remunerated to manage complexity on behalf of customers and has a product availability model that allows for good customization. Sales growth through product line expansion will inevitably drive complexity and costs. Without proper contribution margins and conscious management for simplicity, the top line expansion will become a problem that saps away profitability very quickly.

The best set of tools I've encountered to deal with these challenges are derived from the four natural principles above and fused into a single methodology called "80/20". I chose to call it 80/20 Business Process Improvement (80/20 BPI) for two reasons: (1) the methodology starts with the 80/20 thinking and (2) it's similar to (but different from) other 80/20 methodologies in use today. The key differences are in the implementation phases and in the tools, since the tools support three additional natural laws on top of the 80/20 rule — simplification, fractal, and evolution.

This book is not an implementation manual or a packaged formula used in exactly the same way by successful companies. It has its own cadence and toolbox. Managers need to use critical thinking to decide what, where, and how to apply the methodology. On the other hand, because the natural laws are the building blocks for all these BPI methodologies, there are many things in common among these companies' methods. Primarily they are all thinking processes, not execution cookbooks. They're all focused on how to achieve more with less and move resources from low-value to high-value activities. They also focus on simplification and complexity reduction to be able to care for the vital few and weed out the trivial many. Segmentation and market-focused BUs are also common themes within these companies, as is innovation.

At the end, all of these great companies have unique formulas based on natural laws that cannot be easily replicated. They are all focused on creating and maintaining their economic moats. They want to be radically different from their competitors. Yes, they care about revenue growth, but not at any price. They are far more concerned about ROS (Return on Sales) growth and improving their margins continuously to be able to fund future expansion and create new value for everyone. That is what ITW has done over the years.

When John Nichols came to ITW in 1980, he started a new era of growth and profitability through diversification and acquisitions. He had to create an operating model that would work well among very different businesses under a very decentralized management structure. That model was the 80/20 business methodology. He and the ITW team went looking for companies that fit a set of criteria and that were capable of adding value using the 80/20 methodology with lots of autonomy. This was ITW's formula for handling growth and keeping complexity away. Nichols knew by heart the value of delegation and simplicity after working for years at Ford and ITT.

ITW developed their version of 80/20 business methodology, called the ITW Toolbox, in order to cope with their highly decentralized management structure and their ambitious acquisition program. The process began to gain momentum after Nichols became CEO in 1982 and faced strong competition from Japanese manufacturers. 80/20 started as a product profitability analysis at ITW and slowly evolved into a complete toolbox that was applicable to all company areas and BUs. The ITW Toolbox based on 80/20 brought in a true revolution in terms of mind-sets and management practices within the company. It not only became a tool for M&A and portfolio analysis but also drove away complexity costs and turned poorly performing businesses into manageable and thriving units. Over the years, it became embedded into ITW's culture.

"With all the success ITW has had over the years, Nichols was often asked if there was a manual that people could use to spread the word on 80/20. To everyone's surprise, Nichols would answer there was no manual:

> *I said this over and over again until people were tired of it. Employing 80/20 was a thinking process and I never saw it implemented the same way twice. You couldn't come in with a cookie cutter. If you didn't think through it carefully, you'd make a mistake. I had a three-pager that I used to apply 80/20 to different BUs, and I used that three-pager for fifteen years. Everyone wanted to turn it into a formula and we would sit and argue and we'd say, we don't have a formula! You have to think through your product, market, and technology, and simplify the focus to the primary drivers to make that entity succeed."* [iv]

After working for The Marmon Group, I moved on to different companies, carrying along my own set of beliefs in the natural laws and a new set of 80/20 tools. With several subsequent applications, I kept adjusting and experimenting with different forms of 80/20, using the natural laws to create new approaches. I started to form my own ideas about what works best and which tools are most effective depending on the nature of the business.

These highly connected natural laws are always there, working day and night, just like the law of gravity. And since they work in the same manner every time and everywhere, the Pareto principle, the law of simplicity, the law of fractal behavior, and the law of evolution form the framework for the application of the 80/20 BPI. What I will try to do in this book is to give you an idea about the thinking and the tools so you can deploy this powerful process in your organization. This book refers to tools and uses examples that are based on my manufacturing and industrial engineering background, but the four natural laws and the tools here have no single or distinct realm of application.

For clarity and honesty of purpose, I will remain focused on manufacturing, which is the type of business I know best. But without a doubt, the 80/20 BPI can and is used in almost all business segments, such as services and software, for example. Let me now expand a little on these vital few natural laws that are always in the background of every business.

# CHAPTER 1
## THE VITAL FEW NATURAL LAWS

*In every business, as in every life, there are only a handful of things that matter most. Find out what they are and thrive by allowing them to work for you! Ignore them, and they will work against you!*

The idea that economic events are influenced by natural laws is an old and somewhat controversial idea. Plenty of writers and economists have labored on this. Among them is Henry George,[v] an American writer, politician, and political economist, who was the most influential proponent of the land value tax and the value capture of land and natural resource rents, an idea known at the time as single tax. "Henry George saw the importance of natural law in connection with political economy and human behavior and that it does not only operate in the material world. He goes on to show how it operates through the subtle worlds in which man wills, thinks, and desires and which are critical to the social aspects of human nature and the production and distribution of wealth throughout society."[vi]

*"Probably the most familiar example of the inviolable nature of a natural law is the one that we call "the law of gravity"—it operates irrespective of whether humans acknowledge or ignore it. Human well being is however clearly affected by the extent to which such a law is understood, described, and taken into account in the adjustments human beings make. When humans fly neither human nature nor the law of gravity cease to operate, but conscious human adjustments have been made to accommodate them. When an infant loses a toy because it falls from its grasp he or she begins the learning process—it may take a Newton and then an Einstein to describe the law*

*more fully and inspire more refined adjustments of human behavior, but every baby child learns to acknowledge and work in harmony with the same law.*[vii]

We can point to a number of writers enumerating different natural laws and their impacts on human activities, including Adam Smith. For the most part, they cover a broad spectrum from basic human relationship principles, as in the golden rule, all the way to biological and physical laws, such as the law of entropy. Other principles and economic theories are close to being called natural laws, considering they are so widely accepted in business, such as the law of supply and demand. Although this basic economic theory defining the relationship between demand, supply, and price is well confirmed and understood, it's not actually a natural law but rather a direct consequence of other behaviors in nature. Even though Adam Smith has called it the "natural law of supply and demand," he goes on to mention that it "presupposed predictable patterns of human economic behavior,"[viii] which in its turn can be associated with more basic natural laws, such as efficiency through simplicity and self-repeating or fractal patterns.

Economic principles and natural laws are also embedded in almost all business processes improvement (BPI) methodologies. When we compare a few of the most widely accepted BPI methodologies, as shown in table 1, we keep coming back to a few basic behaviors and patterns associated with each primary work step.

Commonly used business process improvement (BPI) methods:

| PRIMARY WORK STEP | SIX SIGMA (DMAIC) | LEAN | DEMING CYCLE (PDCA) | BUSINESS PROCESS REENGINEERING |
|---|---|---|---|---|
| **DATA DRIVEN ANALYSIS** | Define the problem | Asses the flow (Value Stream Mapping) | Plan (analyze) | Vision and objectives |
| | Measure the current process | | | Identify slacking processes |
| **PROBLEM SOLVING** | Analyze and identify the cause of the problem | Future state mapping | Do (action, take steps under controlled circumstances) | Understand and measure the red processes |
| | | Prioritize opportunities | | |
| **SOLUTION SELECTION** | Improve (implement and verify the solution) | Kaizen (implement change and re-measure) | Check (study the results) | Test and prototype |
| **SUSTAINING** | Control (maintain the solution) | Sustain gains | Act (improve or standardize the process) | Adapt the organization |

Table 1.

All of these improvement methodologies are built on natural cycles of problem recognition, healing, and improvement, which we can easily relate to since we all have similar experiences when we are faced with a personal problem of some magnitude. Before solving a problem, we ask questions and try to understand the nature and complexity of the issue. We instinctively prioritize issues by focusing on large ones first and putting aside minor problems for a while. We then explore multiple alternatives, and once there is a viable solution, we look for ways to apply it with the least effort possible. As the problem is solved, we learn from it and use this experience to either avoid the problem altogether in the future or to solve it faster next time. In either case, we have reached a new level of performance through innovation and moved on to a new baseline.

Four natural laws are contained in this cycle: (1) the law of the vital few and the trivial many, (2) the law of simplicity, (3) the law of fractal behavior, and (4) the law of evolution. We may not be able to entirely rationalize or even recognize their impact on everyday activities, but that does not mean they are not there. The fact that we can easily relate to these methods in business or in our personal lives is due to an intrinsic harmony and natural simplicity in the way they work together. Time over time, this sequence is used to fix and improve businesses everywhere. First, understand and find out what is important (the vital few) and what is not important (the trivial many). Second, simplify and eliminate what doesn't matter (for example, waste). Third, amplify what is good and important (best practices). Fourth, innovate and start this virtuous circle at a higher level of performance (transformational growth).

Unlike the law of supply and demand, the Pareto principle, best known as the 80/20 rule or the law of the vital few and the trivial many, is considered a natural law since it can be observed both in nature and in human activity, not just in economics. Although the exact numbers in the Pareto ratio rarely add up to a hundred, we find plenty of examples in the physical world showing that only a small number of contributors produce the majority of the results—for example, only a small number of countries hold the majority of global oil reserves in the world.

The connection between the major BPI work steps and the natural laws is shown on table 2 below.

| PRIMARY BPI WORK STEP | NATURAL LAW | CONNECTION |
|---|---|---|
| DATA-DRIVEN ANALYSIS | PARETO LAW | Understand the problem using 80/20 principles - the vital few and the trivial many. |
| PROBLEM SOLVING | SIMPLICITY | Optimize, declutter and simplify. |
| SOLUTION SELECTION | FRACTAL | Replicate best patterns, and intensify the best practices. |
| SUSTAINING | EVOLUTION | Reach a new baseline via innovation, and evolve to attain a new performance level. |

Table 2.

At the heart of the matter is the fact that life is not balanced. Life, as well as business, is actually lopsided. If you tap into the vital few inputs or the beneficial side of the law, you will spend less and get more done. However, if you stick with the trivial many and neglect the vital few, you will be exposed to the perverse side of the law. Returning to our example with gravity, there are several good things from the existence of this natural force, such as providing stability to keep us firmly planted on the surface of the earth. This benefit can be exploited for such activities as building structures on the surface of planet. At the same time, there can be hazardous consequences if one ignores the perverse effects of gravity, such as free fall if you cannot offset or soften the gravitational pull when jumping from a high place.

The consequences of ignoring natural laws and adopting artificial methods in economic affairs are devastating. Throughout history there are innumerable examples that turned out very badly for the people involved. Government incentives and subsidies are common artificial mechanisms used to create demand and stimulate economies, sometimes with the best intentions. Unfortunately, many times these artificial means are used to gain political favors in the short-term and end up on the perverse side of natural laws. GSI (the Global Subsidies Initiative) points to two powerful examples in the US economy:

*"Healthy companies depend upon sound business models in a competitive environment. Lousy companies that are limping along on subsidies will slow the growth of the industry. If a product is well designed and meets the needs of the consumer, it will find success in a market economy. In that same market, the real costs of the product are accounted for in a company's profit margin. That is not true of traditional energy companies. Complex and arcane tax laws are used to subsidize these corporations and obscure the true cost of energy. Government subsidies effectively transfer a portion of the costs to taxpayers, enabling artificially low prices and inflated profits."*

*"Many subsidies are defended as benefiting disadvantaged groups, or groups the politicians like to make us believe are disadvantaged. Recently, for example, the Environmental Working Group, an American nonprofit organization, counted up all the direct payments made by the US government to farmers between 1994 and 2005 and found that 10 percent of subsidy recipients collected 73 percent of all subsidies, amounting to $120.5 billion. Analyses of agricultural support programs in other countries appear to lend credence to the 80/20 rule—the impression that 80 percent of support goes to 20 percent of the beneficiaries."*[ix]

In this case, there is not only the issue of bad policy but also the emergence of unintended consequences, created by ignoring the existence of natural laws in economics. We have, in the farming example above, provoked the perverse side of the 80/20 rule.

PEDRO FERRO

## The Vital Few and the Trivial Many (80/20 Rule)

The 80/20 rule is extensively applied in business today in many different ways. In 1941, the great quality consultant guru Joseph Juran named this heuristic principle after its Italian proposer Vilfredo Pareto.[x] In this simple rule, Juran recognized a powerful business tool that helped ignite the quality revolution in Japan during the mid-1950s. The principle is also known by a few other names, including the law of the vital few and the trivial many, the principle of imbalance, and the principle of factor sparsity.

In a nutshell, the principle states that, for many events, roughly 80 percent of the effects come from 20 percent of the causes. As in nature, there are countless areas where this natural law can be observed in business:

- 80 percent of sales revenue comes from 20 percent of customers
- 80 percent of profits come from 20 percent of products
- 80 percent of sales are generated by 20 percent of the sales team
- 80 percent of material purchases come from 20 percent of suppliers
- 80 percent of quality defects come from 20 percent of the causes

When the exact amount of both effort and result can be quantified, it may turn out to be that 24 percent of the effort created 78 percent of the result. It may not add up to 100 percent, but there will almost always be a clear imbalance. As a matter of fact, it will be incredibly unusual to find a perfectly balanced situation where results and efforts turn out to be approximately the same. This observation implies that not all things are equal in business and that some inputs can generate far better results than others. This is consistent with the accepted notion that people, decisions, products, and customers are not all the same. Some have a lot more firepower than others. Some customers, for example, are more equal than others.

The implication of the 80/20 principle is that when two sets of cause and effect data are compared and analyzed, there is a high probability that the results will show a pattern of inequality. From a time-management and resource-allocation point of view, it means one of two things: either time is being spent on things that really matter, or time is being wasted on things that do not make much difference in the scheme of things. Spreading your attention evenly over the total number of inputs is not the optimal way to achieve the best outputs. Either you have the ability to select the vital few, or you will be wasting time and resources by working on the trivial many.

An interesting application of this principle for leaders and knowledge workers is the ninety-six-minute rule, which recommends that you should set aside ninety-six minutes each day without interruptions or distractions to perform your most productive work. Randy Mayeux, a corporate trainer, devised the rule by calculating 20 percent of an eight-hour workday, similar to what Peter Drucker calls "ninety minutes of thinking time." [xi] It is the smallest effective time period required for meaningful knowledge work.

There is a period of time during the day of approximately ninety-six minutes when you are your most productive self. If you can find out when that is and fully concentrate on your most important work while avoiding distractions such as phone calls, e-mails, and other multitasking activities, you will generate the most impactful and productive work of the day. I believe we all have personal experience of this natural phenomenon. After you are done with the focused time, which is 20 percent of your workday, you can be sure you will have accomplished 80 percent of your day's objectives.

Vilfredo Pareto developed this natural principle into the fields of microeconomics and statistics, leaving a strong legacy for future generations. His economic theories are still useful today, and his basic law of the vital few and the trivial many will continue to stimulate the thought processes of many generations to come. And just like it inspired Juran in 1941, the 80/20 principle has inspired and influenced a lot of smart business people throughout the years to create methodologies that are capable of significantly improving business performance.

Many of these performance improvement methodologies inspired by Pareto have received the 80/20 label. Whenever I refer to 80/20 going forward in this book, I am pointing to the many business tools and methodologies that were inspired by the four natural laws and further developed by a number of different business people. I believe that these methods and the tools bundled under the 80/20 methodology name are by far the most effective set of tools available.

The two sides of the 80/20 principle are as follows:

| BENEFICIAL SIDE | PERVERSE SIDE |
|---|---|
| If you work on the vital few things that matter most, you will tip the scale of the natural imbalance on your favor. By isolating the vital few from the trivial many and by increasing your focus on the 20 percent that create 80 percent, you will boost your outcomes significantly. | Ignoring the 80/20 laws and focusing on the trivial many will not only diminish your results but also destroy any business over time. |

## The Law of Simplicity

The law of simplicity in nature and in economics is tightly connected to the 80/20 principle. One can say that 80/20 helps identify the vital few and the law of simplicity helps deal with the trivial many. As John Maeda defines in his book The Laws of Simplicity, simplicity is about "subtracting the obvious and adding the meaningful."xii Simplicity equals sanity in the sense that you are not allowing the trivial many to drive your attention away from the vital few. Every time you do extra activities or transactions to accomplish the same results, you are not only being unproductive but also creating complexity in the business and turning your back on the natural law of simplicity. Unwanted and unpaid complexity can make the business unsustainable over time. Compliance with the law of simplicity in the context of 80/20 means to work diligently on complexity reduction and make sure that complexity does not creep into the business without being allowed to do so.

> *That's been one of my mantras—focus and simplicity. Simple can be harder than complex. You have to work hard to get your thinking clean to make it simple. But it's worth it in the end because once you get there you can move mountains.*
>
> *-- Steve Jobs*

Simplicity is ubiquitous in the natural world, even though we may see a lot of complexity everywhere. The fact that we have a limited understanding of most natural occurrences does not mean they are inherently complex. Today we understand and predict the behavior of many natural phenomena with simple, general laws of physics, for example. The law of gravity is a good example of a complex phenomenon made simple to understand and predict using physics to uncover simplicity.

The nineteenth-century philosopher Henry David Thoreau wrote quite a lot about simplicity, and this passage in particular is strongly linked to 80/20 thinking: "I do believe in simplicity. It is astonishing as well as sad, how many trivial affairs even the wisest thinks he must attend to in a day; how singular an affair he thinks he must omit. When the mathematician would solve a difficult problem, he first frees the equation of all encumbrances, and reduces it to its simplest terms. So simplify the problem of life, distinguish the necessary and the real. Probe the earth to see where your main roots run."[xiii]

Unwanted and unmanaged complexity can ruin a business by creating too much cost and overhead. Very profitable businesses do not need much overhead to operate. It is not that additional growth and scale are bad things. Revenue growth is important and is strongly correlated with profitability. The problem is when additional complexity in the forms of added transactions, facilities, systems, and people comes along with the additional revenue. To make matters worse, complexity management is not a hot topic in most companies or in business schools. Managers have a natural tendency to ignore complexity, sometimes until it is too late to reduce. In some cases, complexity is regarded and used as a form of job security.

A lot of complexity that goes unmeasured or unmanaged in the organization is created when companies embark on revenue growth at any cost. In most cases, this occurs when companies grow their product and customer portfolios in mature, developed mass markets without considering the 80/20 principles and without strategizing to keep complexity at bay. Growth on many different small fronts, without segmentation and focus, creates a lot of new transactions and increases costs much more than profits.

Optimizing portfolios and production lines, streamlining business processes, and segmenting BUs are some of the tools used by the 80/20 improvement process to reduce complexity. As mentioned in Thoreau's quote above, one of the best approaches to deal with a complex problem is to reduce it to its simplest terms, breaking it into smaller pieces to understand each individual piece as well as how they all work together.

There are two sides to the law of simplicity:

| BENEFICIAL SIDE | PERVERSE SIDE |
| --- | --- |
| Simplicity basically pays off to the bottom line by allowing you to do more with less. It brings sanity to the business by weeding out the trivial many and by letting the sun shine on the vital few. | If you do nothing, complexity will creep into the business and eat away the profitability. You need to be alert and prepared to fight complexity with proactive simplicity. Sometimes you need a chief simplification officer. |

### The Law of Fractal Behavior

*Clouds are not spheres, mountains are not cones, coastlines are not circles, and bark is not smooth, nor does lightning travel in a straight line.*

*—Benoit B. Mandelbrot*

A fractal is a "never ending pattern that repeats itself at different scales. This property is called self-similarity."[xiv] Fractals occur very often in nature and can be observed in trees, forests, river networks, blood vessels, etc. The fractal behavior in business, as applied to 80/20 methodologies, can be understood as the tendency of markets to evolve and grow upstream and downstream of a reference segment while maintaining self-similar features among the customers in either direction.

As you closely examine the details of an existing market, you will find endless segments, or customer groupings, sharing similar patterns among themselves and yet being connected to the original segment in some way. The same can be observed when you take a step back and see that the macro behaviors of a group of markets follow certain predictable patterns even though they look quite different on the surface. To use an analogy to Mandelbrot's quote, the markets we serve do not really exist in the way we conceive them. But even though there may be infinite ways we can combine customers and define new segments, there will always be similar clusters up or down the market that we can use to isolate coherent sectors. It all depends on the focus of the person looking into the microscope.

The fractal analogy also helps us understand that markets will show unpredictable behaviors, which can be entirely unexpected and border on the edge of chaos. We've come to expect a certain outcome from a market based on our interaction with a group of customers with similar features, however changes in characteristics not completely known to us may cause ripple effects and change the entire structure of the market at once. This is, by the way, what happens frequently in the technology markets. A disruptive technology used by a segment of the market can cause the entire market to change in a short period of time. This is what happened with the advent of social networks, which started in a micro segment of the market and are now a major disruptive force and a threat to voice and even e-mail communications.

Market segments are never stagnant and never completely separate from other sectors of the broader market. If you study specific groupings of customers, you will always find niches or subsegments that contain the same basic elements of the broader market and yet have unique characteristics of their own. You will always be able to look into a segment with different eyes and find new patterns. 80/20 leverages this natural behavior by taking a snapshot of a market segment at a given time and applying extreme focus to understand the self-similarities and patterns to de-average or specialize products and services, capturing more value from the vital few customers and products. From time to time, this exercise needs to be repeated as markets are always changing.

The downstream and upstream segmentation approach is key to attain focus and growth. The same mind-set also brings a lot more objectivity to the mission of finding the right customer or market groups that are in line with your unique value proposition (UVP). It helps companies avoid selling their products and services to customers that are not their primary targets. Segmentation and specialization are key to taking advantage of the natural fractal behavior, reducing or weeding out the trivial many activities that only drive more complexity into the business.

Beyond finding target segments for sales and marketing purposes, 80/20 uses fractal behavior and segmentation as a management discipline. It makes the market-segment-focused BU into the heart and soul of the organization. It deploys empowered and autonomous leadership to look into the microscope and lead the organization to better serve well-defined clusters of customers until it is time to segment again.

Here are the two sides of the law of fractal behavior:

| BENEFICIAL SIDE | PERVERSE SIDE |
|---|---|
| If you are prepared to understand the self-similarities among your "eighty" customers, a subsegment of the vital few will always yield better results than the collection of all the trivial many in the same or a new market, with a lot less effort. | If you don't take the time to understand the fractal nature of your vital few customers and their self-similarities, you will be led in the wrong direction when looking for growth. |

## The Law of Evolution

*It is not the strongest or the most intelligent who will survive but those who can best manage change.*

—*Leon C. Megginson*

"Evolution is defined as the process of growth and development or the theory that organisms have grown and developed from past organisms."[xv] We have plenty of evolution examples in all fields of human activity, mainly in science and technology. Charles Darwin developed the theory of evolution as applied to living organisms. He uncovered the law of evolution by natural selection, which basically states that growth and evolution are inevitable for all living species. He also described the way species grow through natural selection and gradualism. Adaptability and continuous improvement of the species is key for survival and advancement.

Growth and evolution are equally mandatory for every economy, marketplace, or business to survive and thrive. Countries need to grow to improve the quality of life of their citizens. Companies need to grow to respond to the evolving needs of their markets and stakeholders. Once a company is launched, there is no going back—it is only forward, or eventually the company will die. Individuals will die anyway, but the species will continue to move forward and evolve. Evolution is inevitable.

Innovation is the driving force behind evolution in business, as it defines new levels of performance and elevates the baseline for organizations. It is the result of learning combined with deliberate thinking to solve problems and to find answers to unmet needs. In my personal experience, character and learning come with suffering and pain. Pain and pleasure are natural forces that compel us to find solutions. I don't mean pleasure in the sense of immediate gratification, although that may be the case, but long-term pleasure that leads us to a happier future state.

The 80/20 methodology sees two different categories of innovation: (1) segment-focused or applied innovation and (2) systematic innovation. Segment-focused or applied innovation is driven by BUs and is generally directed at products and commercial practices. This type of innovation is incremental in nature and used to remove obstacles and solve problems for markets and customers, allowing them to evolve as well. It is focused on either removing pain or on satisfying a real need from the market.

Systematic innovation is strategic in nature and goes well beyond product invention and new ideas related to business practices. It looks to innovate in more than one dimension at a time, such as in business processes, product offerings, delivery processes, and financial systems. The goal of systematic innovation is to create value for customers and stakeholders over time by creating what Warren Buffett calls a wide economic moat to protect a company from existing and new competition.

As with evolutionary strategies in nature, we can see the need for both defensive (segment-focused) and offensive (systematic) innovation in order to develop a wide economic moat, which will defend the core business and lead to transformational growth. Innovation is not a matter of choice but a matter of change.

There are two sides to the law of evolution:

| BENEFICIAL SIDE | PERVERSE SIDE |
|---|---|
| Innovating on your business model as you grow is far less risky than trying to add more revenues and complexity on top of the same old model. Innovation is a powerful growth fuel when it is focused on the path of the vital few. | If you don't evolve and grow, you will not stay stable. You will actually shrink, becoming a prey to your competitors. Without relevant innovation, the business will stagnate and eventually die. |

These four natural laws or principles are highly interconnected and function as the ecosystem or the background to implement the 80/20 BPI. If one of them is disrespected, it can render the process ineffective and create troubles, very much like when someone disregards the law of gravity when trying to take flight. At a high level, the combination of these four laws tells us to work diligently to find out what drives the business and what creates complexity. Once you've identified these drivers, you should look for more of the good and weed out the bad.

Through understanding the fractal behavior in the market, you can focus on areas that give you the most growth and profitability. You will be looking for those customer groupings and segments that value your products and services more than the whole of the market. The understanding also means that you will not waste effort on customers and markets that are not likely to care about your UVP. Once you've acquired focus, then it is time to evolve and innovate, creating your moat and defending your sustainability.

The Pareto principle is a powerful natural law, but it is not the whole of the 80/20 business process improvement (BPI) methodology. To make it happen, you need to combine understanding about the vital few natural laws with 80/20 thinking and 80/20 tools.

# CHAPTER 2
# 80/20 THINKING

What I consider 80/20 thinking is a form of critical thinking process and an attitude focused on searching for imbalance coupled with a passion for simplicity. Disproportionally talented people, above-average products, unique customer relationships, and uncommon cost advantages are all examples of imbalances. Most of the time, these are so close to us that we fail to notice how exceptional they are. I believe that no activity escapes one of the most basic laws of nature: the law of the vital few and the trivial many. It's about being a lot more selective and a lot less exhaustive, knowing that all resources, tools, and people do not have the same value. They are different, and they produce significantly different results, depending on the situation. These exceptional resources are the outliers in a world full of mediocrity.

The attitude and the mind-set to embrace exceptional performance may come naturally, but the selective part is not always intuitive. It requires critical thinking. You need data and information coupled with discernment to make clear and rational decisions driven by evidence. This mental process uses many skills, including analysis, synthesis, knowledge application, and some level of intuition, to reach an answer or conclusion. So you need to be sensitive to exceptional performance, but you also need to crunch the numbers. But collecting relevant information for data analysis is not always easy, since there is never enough intelligence of the right quality to support critical thinking: there is either too much useless data cluttering the field or not enough facts of the right kind to lean on. This is the reality in business, as it is in life. Life is unfair. Unless you invest an enormous amount of time and money researching, gathering, and validating the data, chances are that you will have to make decisions based on imperfect and insufficient information.

According to one definition, critical thinking involves problem solving, decision-making, metacognition, rational thinking, reasoning, knowledge, intelligence and also a moral component such as reflective thinking. Critical thinkers therefore need to have reached a level of maturity in their development, possessing a certain attitude as well as a set of taught skills. Even though this definition starts with a list of high-level abilities, at the end it suggests that, in order to have good critical thinking skills, you need to work hard at developing them. Attaining critical thinking requires continuous practice paired with genuine curiosity and an open mind. Knowing where to find knowledge (metacognition) is important, but most essential is a healthy attitude toward finding reality, whatever reality is, coupled with a certain dose of humility to allow the data to speak for itself. In other words, to let the data talk, you have to be willing to accept that facts are friendly, and put your ego aside. The facts will not mislead or lie to you.

The 80/20 BPI combines pure thought and critical thinking into a simple and yet powerful way to reach answers and conclusions through objective analysis. It's simple because it considers the limitations of working with less than perfect sets of data. It's powerful because it accounts for the natural imbalances in business to save time and resources. It's also practical because it comes with a toolbox to help with the analysis and with the implementation of the methodology. As with many tools, it needs to be applied with common sense to facilitate critical thinking and not as a way to replace critical thinking and common sense. But you shouldn't look at 80/20 as a tactical tool only since it embodies the most strategic elements, such as continued value creation and resource optimization. The experience of and real world results from the application of 80/20 thinking and methodologies speak for themselves, when you evaluate the historical performance of companies that use both the mind-set and the BPI.

If we accept this natural principle and recognize that business is full of asymmetric situations, we have to ask the question: How come managers don't use these imbalances more often to make decisions? For example, why wouldn't a businessperson concentrate the majority of a company's capital and talent to support the 20 percent of the customers and products that generate 80 percent of the profits instead of diluting efforts and resources across the entire field?

There are two possible answers. The first lies with the fact that managers are not trained to be selective but to be exhaustive. They think about 100 percent of the inputs and results 100 percent of the time. They try to cover all the bases, and they often fail in critical areas by not addressing the favorable imbalances first. These misses can often be attributed to the reverse side of 80/20, where 80 percent of the failure is a direct result of a 20 percent effort in the wrong direction.

The second reason is due to the fact that managers do not always allow the data to talk and point them in the right direction. Paradoxically, I believe that the excessive amount of data and information generated by modern data management systems has reduced the analytical ability of organizations. Managers rely too much on packaged data systems that are designed to treat all transactions as equal.

Thinking about imbalances is not always natural—it doesn't come instinctively to everyone. Most of the time, it needs to be exercised and primed with data analytics. People who are 80/20 thinkers have developed the ability to formulate estimations about possible imbalances between inputs and outputs. They visualize a mental ratio between effort and result, and then they follow a hunch to determine and pursue what matters most. They also work diligently to stay focused on the vital few while avoiding being sucked into the world of the trivial many. And in life and in business, 80 percent of the time you will be bombarded by trivial issues.

80/20 thinking implies that we should do the following:

1. Incentivize and focus on exceptional gains and results instead of scattering your efforts throughout a larger number of small initiatives that will bring incremental results across the board. An example is Google's "10x" mentality:

   *"The philosophy of "10x" is woven into Google's DNA. Instead of improving something by 10 percent, the company strives to work on projects that are 10 times better than anything else out there. "A big part of my job is to get people focused on things that are not just incremental," CEO Larry Page told Wired in 2013. Getting to chase big ideas instead of simply one-upping competitors is one of the best parts about working for the company, employees have said. That mindset has launched some of Google's most amazingly ambitious projects, like self-driving cars, Internet-bearing balloons, and magnetic nanoparticles that can search the human body for disease."*

*"But the 10x mentality also ushered in now-established products like Gmail—which initially gave users 100 times more storage than any other product out there and was seen as a crazy digression by people who only thought of Google as a search company—and Google Street View, which has photographed more than 7.2 million miles of road. Right at the roots, Google's early search engine was a 10x manifestation of the web annotation tool Page was working on as a thesis project at Stanford."*[xvi]

2. Search hard for ways to bootstrap your projects early on by focusing on a limited number of initiatives. Bootstrapping means using your own resources or operating revenues from the business to fund the project. In most cases, managers will resort to conventional ways to do things in order to reduce risk and cover all angles up front instead of focusing on the end goal. An example is GoPro Inc., a maker of HD personal cameras.

*Rather than developing new technology up front and going after venture capital moneys to launch his company, Nick Woodman thought of unconventional ways to apply and package existing camera and data storage technologies, focusing on "high-adrenaline sports" market segments, such as skydiving, base jumping and white-water rafting. This approach was much more cost effective and kept the company from going after private equity money early on, which would have been a distraction. By limiting the scope at the beginning of the project, it helped bootstrap the company to have early successes that Nick was able to build upon.*

3. Choose your battles well and concentrate on winning them. Let others fight the myriad of small battles in the war. As many in 80/20 say, "be selective, not exhaustive." An example is Netflix, Inc.:

*"After CEO Reed Hastings made up his mind about where he would focus the company in the long run, he dropped everything else to build the new business. Including his legacy business of mailing DVDs to people's homes. In classic 80/20 thinking, he selected his "80 strategy" and started to "milk" his 20 business to fund the 80. He shifted resources and focus to the 80 strategy."*

*"In 2011, he split Netflix into 2 businesses—DVD and*

*streaming—and allowed them to price independently and compete with each other for customer business. He was trounced as the "dunce" of tech CEOs. His actions led to a price increase of 60 percent for anyone who decided to buy both Netflix products, and many customers chose to drop one. Analysts predicted this to be the end of Netflix. But in retrospect we can see the brilliance of this decision. CEO Hastings actually did what textbooks tell us to do—he began milking the installed, but outdated, DVD business. He did not kill it, but he began pulling profits and cash out of it to pay for building the faster growing, but lower margin, streaming business. This allowed Netflix to actually grow revenue, and grow profits, while making the market transition from one platform (DVD) to another (streaming)."*

*"When you need to move into a new market, set up a new division to attack it. And give them permission to do whatever it takes, even if their actions aggravate existing customers and industry participants. Push them to learn fast, and grow fast—and even to attack old sacred cows (like bundled pricing)."*[xvii]

4.  Work diligently to identify, attract, and create opportunities for people who can think and act according to 80/20 principles. Then delegate the work and support them in their mission:

    *The people that can think 80/20 and leverage imbalances need more than a conventional job or career path. Choose them wisely! They need to be in positions that are impactful, such as running business units, and to be made accountable for the results. They thrive on challenges. If you do a great job selecting "80 people", then you are better off adopting a supportive leadership style and virtually working for them and concentrating yourself on what you do best. Let them do the work for you and focus on making them happy. They are the actual "vital few", and they will have a positive multiplying influence on your bottom line.*

5.  Have fun, do what you love, and ensure your team enjoys what they are doing. Richard Branson[xviii] said it best:

    *"Fun is one of the most important and underrated components of any successful venture. If you're not enjoying yourself, it's probably time to call it quits and try something else. If your employees are engaged and*

*having fun, and they genuinely care about your customers, they will enjoy their work more and do a better job. Hire people who look for the best in others, who lavish more praise than they dole out criticism, and who genuinely love what they do."*[xix]

# CHAPTER 3
# THE 80/20 MODEL

*In business, I look for economic castles protected by unbreachable moats.*

*—Warren Buffett*

The 80/20 methodology is a proven and broadly used approach, and in almost all successful applications, we can find at least three things in common: First and foremost, 80/20 thinking and confidence in the process are present throughout the organization. Second, there is an implementation cycle, or a number of phases that are followed in sequence. Third, there are specific methods or tools that are well understood and are applied at each phase of the process (a toolbox). These three elements combined lead to successful applications.

The implementation cycle is a coherent succession of phases that have worked well together over time: the four phases are (A) analysis, (S) simplification, (F) focus, and (G) growth. From now on, I will refer to this implementation cycle as the ASFG cycle. It's also not a coincidence that it can resemble the Deming or PDSA cycle, which was later called the PDCA (plan, do, check, and act) cycle. Both have a similar goal defined as "a systematic series of steps for gaining valuable learning and knowledge for the continual improvement of a product or process."[xx] Each of these four steps is closely linked to the vital few natural laws, as well as the 80/20 principle. The ASFG cycle is represented on figure 1 below.

**The ASFG implementation cycle:**

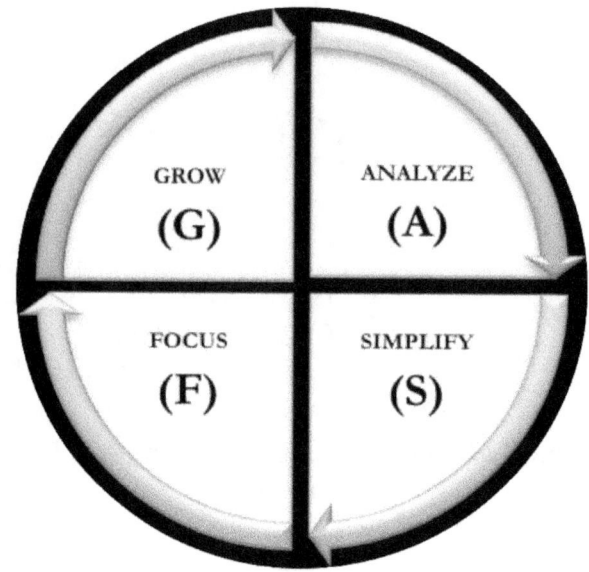

Figure 1.

To follow the ASFG cycle means that you start by organizing raw data and analyzing the information at hand, allowing the data to talk. Once it does and reveals any hidden complexities, you can move on to reduce complexity in the product portfolio, administrative processes, manufacturing operation, or performance management metrics. Only after simplification can you segment the business to increase focus and to fully capture new revenue and profit streams. With segmentation focus and specialization of your unique value proposition, you evolve and grow through product, process, and design innovation and new business platforms. And then you start all over again.

The simple but effective exercise of data analytics built on the 80/20 thinking is very powerful. It increases the level of management confidence to proceed with changes and reveals nuances and relationships that otherwise remain dormant in the raw data. I am always amazed by how simple yet effective and awesome this process really is. It can be so counterintuitive at times that you have to keep drilling into the data until you finally decide to give up on previous hypotheses or biases that existed in the pure thinking. That is when the data talks.

The outcome of the analytics should point you in the direction of the "eighty" and give you a picture of the current state of complexity and allocation of efforts and resources. It's powerful because it's simple and also because it gives you immediate opportunities to take action and refocus the business. Once the data talks, it's time to take action. But let me emphasize right away that the actions you take depend on the situation. There is no magic bullet or formulaic approach. There are tools that can be applied depending on each case. By working on the few things that make the "eighty" better, you will give your scarce resources a multiplying effect. And by not allowing the "eighty" to be contaminated with the "twenty's" complexity, you will be releasing the power of focus into the business.

The key requirement as you work through this methodology is that 80/20 thinking be present at all phases of implementation and beyond. Since there is no rigid formula, managers must use 80/20 thinking to discern which tools and decisions provide the best ratio of effort to result at each step. 80/20 is about doing a few things (the vital ones) in the right order. It is acting smart and taking the time to find out what is important before you start working. It is all about simplicity and clarity of purpose. Complexity that does not add value is a huge enemy of this process. If carried along to the next steps, complexity will pollute the "eighty" and dampen the impact of the tools. Only after you've developed a simplification strategy can you think about segmentation for the purposes of separating unlike businesses, or dividing the "eighty" from the "twenty."

The last step is the growth phase, which is when the business maintains the comparative advantage developed in this process via continuous application of 80/20 thinking and through innovation, creating what Warren Buffett calls the moat to keep the competition from attacking the successes. As you would have guessed, 80/20 is an evergreen process. You want to continue to couple the thinking with the analytics as markets change and technologies evolve to create and maintain your moat.

### The 80/20 BPI Toolbox

Now that we have covered the four phases in the implementation cycle, let's look at the tools available at each phase of the process. The ASFG cycle with the respective tools is represented in table 3 below.

**Tools associated with each implementation phase:**

| (A) Analyze | (S) Simplify | (F) Focus | (G) Grow |
|---|---|---|---|
| CP matrix | Product line simplification | Segmentation | Segment-focused innovation |
| Quad analysis | | Business unit formation | |
| | Business process simplification | | Systematic innovation |
| Optimization | | | |
| | Product availability simplification | | |
| | Lean metrics | | |

Table 3.

## Analytics (A)

Data analytics (DA) uses raw data to draw conclusions about information. With the ever-increasing power of information-system resources, DA has become highly desirable, making a lot of money for consulting and IT firms alike. The abundance of data makes it easy to mine for information nuggets to exhaustion. The most sought after data pieces are related to markets, customers, and products, as managers search for new insights into buying patterns and marketing strategies. However, this can be done to a point where too much information becomes a problem and can lead to complexity and paralysis. The law of simplicity must be at play here to bring sanity to this process. The focus has to be on relevant information that can add value to customers, employees, and shareholders.

The 80/20 Customer-Product (CP) matrix is a simple exercise that aims to organize and analyze related data sets that can bring your company's most important activity into focus. This exercise can be compared to a jigsaw puzzle game, since it allows you to visualize complexity and extract essential conclusions that are not so intuitive when you look at individual bits and pieces of the puzzle. The whole is much more meaningful and revealing than the preliminary mental picture we draw in our heads when we start the process. It also gives you the ability to begin adjusting your portfolio right away, so you don't need to wait for the completion of the entire cycle to start seeing results. The matrix is also the best planning tool to use before you decide to move forward with additional tools and take on the next steps. As you will see, this simple analytical tool is useful at each and every stage of the process, but needs to be kept evergreen. It should be constantly recast as the data evolves (every six months or whenever necessary) and, along with the quadrant analysis from the CP matrix, it becomes an excellent visual aid and dashboard for managers to understand how business is changing. I will explain later in the book how to use both the CP matrix and the quadrant analysis.

## Simplification (S)

Reducing complexity through product line simplification and business process simplification.

1. Product line simplification (PLS) is a method to reduce and manage the complexity associated with your product portfolio. We use different simplification strategies for different quadrants of the CP matrix (refer to chapter 4 - 80/20 analytics) and define filters and methods to avoid adding more complexity as the business grow.

2. Business process simplification (BPS) provides a way to remove complexity from business processes. It describes a team approach for developing "is maps" and "should maps" (these tools will be addressed in the BPS section) and using brainstorming techniques to generate ideas and to plan for change. BPS also provides a framework when deciding to automate any process using information technology.

Creating product availability through in-lining and outsourcing, depending on the resulting strategies from the CP matrix analysis. You will select different sources for different types of products, using the following tools:

1. In-lining is a manufacturing approach for your high-volume products using single-piece-flow production lines, grouping machines, and operations in a separate area apart from low-volume products. It drives a lot of complexity away from manufacturing and empowers the shop floor teams to manage their space as a mini business unit. In-lining takes the simplification process a step further by improving the workflow and using market rate of demand (MRD) to pace production.

MRD is a materials management philosophy based on the actual consumption pattern of products imposed by the market. It is a type of simple and visual pull system used for materials replenishment in manufacturing operations and sales organizations. It is primarily applied on high-volume products to eliminate shortages and excesses by removing the use of inaccurate forecasting tools. It helps improve customer service and reduce inventory levels.

2.  Outsourcing is a tool that helps to decide what and when to buy from third-party suppliers to offer a complete portfolio to your customers, rather than manufacturing everything in-house. This initiative reduces complexity and costs while improving your ability to serve your vital few customers.

Using lean metrics to track results, productivity, and complexity. These vital few metrics are designed to reduce management complexity by allowing you to focus on the KPIs (key performance indicators).

1.  Results metrics are the key financial indicators, for example contribution margin (calculated using direct costing), ROS (return on sales) growth, and free cash flow.

2.  Productivity metrics track the ratio between results and effort. A typical metric is called GM2 (gross margin two) and reveals a ratio between total contribution-margin dollars divided by the total payroll dollars for the business unit. GM2 incorporates several important elements, such as the market willingness to pay for the UVP, variable costs required to create product availability and the necessary effort to operate the business, reflected in the total payroll for direct and indirect production workers, and administrative people. Some companies also measure the effectiveness of the efforts to improve the "eighty's" quadrant, in terms of cost, availability, and quality. For example, net material cost savings and optimization of the "eighty" SKUs (stock keeping units) versus the target.

3.  Complexity metrics are also known as the missing metrics because they are rarely tracked by traditional accounting. For example, sales and contribution margin (CM) per SKU, number of SKUs entering and exiting the firm in a given period, cost to set up and maintain an SKU, etc.

## Focus (F)

Market segmentation is a decentralization approach guided by findings from the CP matrix that enables you to create new BUs and to specialize in subsegments of your "eighty" markets. Segmentation's objective is to increase sales, market shares, and profitability by focusing on specific end user markets. It provides the necessary structure (leadership, people, and capital) for BUs to evolve from a commercial only approach into a full profit and loss approach. It is an experiment in growth that takes advantage of the fractal nature of the market.

## Growth (G)

This phase is where you transcend segmentation by using a new approach to innovation. Instead of only product innovation, I will now focus on business design innovation. This is where you venture into new ideas to create your moat from the outside in, as compared to inside out incremental innovation related exclusively to new products. "The term economic moat, coined and popularized by Warren Buffett, refers to a business's ability to maintain competitive advantages over its competitors in order to protect its long-term profits and market share from competing firms."[xxi] The growth phase is where you step out to anticipate and influence change in the marketplace.

When we overlay the implementation cycle on top of the 80/20 thinking and tools, with the vital few natural laws as the background or ecosystem, we have our business model, displayed in figure 2.

**The 80/20 Business Process Improvement model:**

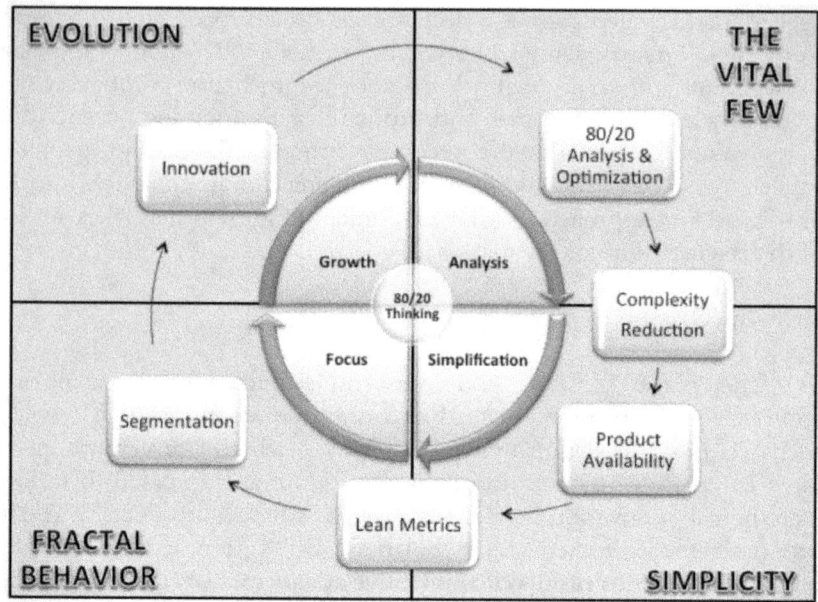

Figure 2.

The 80/20 thinking and the tools, applied in logical sequence, enables management to remain on the beneficial side of the vital few natural laws. In the following chapters, we will review each step of the ASFG cycle and the tools in greater details.

# CHAPTER 4
# 80/20 ANALYTICS

The first stage of the 80/20 business process improvement (BPI) methodology is the analytical phase. It requires that you create a data rich customers and products (CP) matrix to use as a base for developing early strategies to improve sales and contribution margins and to simplify the business. I will explain how to create the CP matrix and how to use it in this chapter.

The work here is to map out and separate the vital few from the trivial many, using data that is most pure and promptly available. Unit volumes and sales revenues by customer and by product are normally available in most companies. Almost always there is also reasonably accurate data on contribution or variable margins, or at a minimum material margins, if contribution or variable margins are not accurate enough or in case they are contaminated with too many arbitrary allocations. Volume and revenue data are normally easier to obtain and, unlike margin data, they normally do not have incorrectly allocated numbers associated with them. They simply tell the story of where the "eighty" and the "twenty" currently are. We need pure, factual data relating to the current level of activity of the business. Revenues carry a high correlation to profits, and number of products and transactions are intrinsically related to complexity and fixed costs.

The matrix is helpful as an approximation of complexity measurement and shows the alignment between resources and activities that generate the most value for businesses, especially for those supporting customers. Only with useful data and enough scrutiny can you begin to understand where the center of gravity is in relation to the application of your company's resources. If you had to serve only one customer with one product, your business would be a lot simpler and easier to manage. The "eighty" of the resources and attention would be directly applied to this one customer and this single product. Everything else would fall under the "twenty" category (the non-mission-critical category).

In the real world, companies are dealing with a multitude of customers and a large number of product lines. This is when the 80/20 principle is most insightful: there will always exist a smaller set of customers and products responsible for the majority of revenues and profits. Not only that, but analytics will show that 80 percent of the growth, profitability, and loyalty come from 20 percent of the clients. Once the vital few customers are identified, the organization needs to shift its focus to provide them with differentiated products and services. The aim is to acquire these customers for life and then bring new ones into the "eighty." To accomplish that, you need to develop the right level of intimacy with these clients, to understand exactly why they buy from you and not from your competitor. And you also need to understand their current and future needs very well. But not all the customers are vital, and not all sales efforts are efficient. Some will not produce any valuable results. So the challenge is to ensure that the best sales efforts and the attention of your best employees are being applied to the right set of customers (the vital few).

Before we go any further, it's important to note that this exercise in data analytics is not exclusive to customers and products; it can be applied to any two sets of interconnected data to understand the 80/20 constituents and to reach conclusions about complexity. Different sets of data are linked in business, such as suppliers and transactions, people and costs, procedures and reports, and so on. There is great value in analyzing different areas for simplification of business processes, for example. We use the customers and products (CP) matrix since it represents the starting point of the methodology and because it contains the two most valuable and interrelated sets of data about the company.

The analytical portion of 80/20 can be broken down in six phases:

1. Deciding what to analyze
2. Gathering the raw data
3. Building the 80/20 matrix
4. Doing the quad analysis
5. Applying optimization strategies
6. Planning for the next phase

## Step 1: Deciding What to Analyze

You can use the CP matrix itself to decide where to apply 80/20 first by segregating the vital few areas of the business. But in most cases, the business needs will drive the target area selection. Groups of people from potential target areas should be involved in the discussion early on with the facilitation of senior management. Some helpful questions to ask in relation to applicable areas are as follows:

- What are the business's needs – what are you trying to improve?
    - Profitability?
    - Quality?
    - Market share?
    - Customer service?
- Which projects are the most promising?
- What areas present too much complexity?
- Which strategic parts of the business can benefit from 80/20?
- Which business units are struggling?

Once you decide where the initial focus should be, the management team of the target area or business should organize the task force that will lead this phase of the process. Outside technical resources (finance and IT, for example) can be used to support the task force, but it is essential that the people managing the target area conduct the analysis.

When planning for the next stage, the task force needs to give some consideration to the level of detail needed to represent each customer and product entry in the matrix. Depending on the purpose of the analysis, you may want to consider breaking down the customer into different entities that are invoiced by the company, for example stores or shipping locations. As for products, it is useful to distinguish the different specifications or part numbers that are actually sold to customers. Granularity helps at the later stages of the analysis. It is useful to start at the macro level and drill down to shipping entities and product specifications later on. Sometimes the level of detail is driven by the quality of the data that is available when you start.

## Step 2: Gathering Data

The next step in the process is to gather interrelated sales data for customers and products using windows of six to twelve months past. A year of data is normally sufficient to account for seasonality. However, businesses that are prone to extreme cycles will require more than one year's worth of data. The objective is to organize the data in such a way that you can see sales or unit volume data at the intersection of each customer and SKU in a spreadsheet.

Depending on whether margin data is readily available or not, it would save time later on to gather contribution margin information for each product sold to each customer. Sometimes the margins are only available at the SKU level (or really do not vary much by customer), which can be good to collect as well. Regardless how detailed the margins are, a judgment call must be made here in regards to the purity of the data. If the variable margin information contains too many allocations (as in a traditional absorption costing methodology), it is better to use a proxy metric for contribution margin, such as direct material margins. Variable margins can be used as long as the data truly reflects the variable components in the making of each respective product: direct material cost, direct labor cost, and direct overhead or manufacturing burden.

The task force may want to have the total dataset for the chosen period of time available in a database or spreadsheet. It should at least contain the following fields:

- Customer name (or customer name and invoice location)
- SKU number
- Total revenue
- Unit volume sold
- Contribution margin (or material margin or value-added margin)

In general, the basic customer data related to sales is shown in terms of revenue, as per table 4. Customers are listed with the associated revenue in descending order, and the cumulative revenue is used to draw the line between "eighty" and "twenty" customers. This type of data set is normally a good indication of the vital few customers, but it is not yet final. For qualitative analysis, we need to keep an open mind and pay attention to the transitional customers and the low-volume customers that may have the potential to become "eighty" customers someday. At the same time, a "twenty" customer could very well be an "eighty" customer for a key competitor.

**80/20 customer revenue data table:**

|  | Customer | Revenue $ | Cumulative $ | Cumulative % |
|---|---|---|---|---|
| Top customers | A | $254,478 | $254,478 | 27% |
|  | B | $205,398 | $459,876 | 49% |
|  | C | $138,711 | $598,587 | 64% |
|  | D | $135,845 | $734,432 | 79% |
| Transitional Customers | E | $32,935 | $767,367 | 82% |
|  | F | $31,356 | $798,723 | 86% |
|  | G | $29,273 | $827,996 | 89% |
| Low-volume customers | H | $26,955 | $854,951 | 92% |
|  | I | $25,862 | $880,813 | 95% |
|  | J | $19,145 | $899,958 | 97% |
|  | K | $16,225 | $916,183 | 98% |
|  | L | $14,345 | $930,528 | 100% |
|  |  | $930,528 |  |  |

Table 4.

Along the same lines, table 5 shows the separate list of all products or SKUs and associated revenue for the selected time window. Here again, we should be careful not to jump to a more definite classification without further analysis and a deeper understanding of market dynamics. A low-volume product for us does not necessarily means a low-volume product for the market as a whole.

**80/20 SKU revenue data table:**

|  | SKU | Revenue $ | Cumulative $ | Cumulative % |
|---|---|---|---|---|
| Top product | 1 | $170,120 | 170,120 | 18% |
|  | 2 | $164,345 | 334,465 | 36% |
|  | 3 | $129,570 | 464,035 | 50% |
|  | 4 | $81,094 | 545,129 | 59% |
|  | 5 | $80,653 | 625,782 | 67% |
|  | 6 | $76,171 | 701,953 | 75% |
| Transitional product | 7 | $70,873 | $772,826 | 83% |
|  | 8 | $33,860 | $806,686 | 87% |
|  | 9 | $32,490 | $839,176 | 90% |
| Low-volume products | 10 | $17,925 | $857,101 | 92% |
|  | 11 | $13,684 | $870,785 | 94% |
|  | 12 | $13,127 | $883,912 | 95% |
|  | 13 | $12,253 | $896,165 | 96% |
|  | 14 | $9,230 | $905,395 | 97% |
|  | 15 | $7,298 | $912,693 | 98% |
|  | 16 | $5,800 | $918,493 | 99% |
|  | 17 | $4,623 | $923,116 | 99% |
|  | 18 | $3,654 | $926,770 | 100% |
|  | 19 | $1,950 | $928,720 | 100% |
|  | 20 | $1,808 | $930,528 | 100% |
|  |  | $930,528 |  |  |

Table 5.

## Step 3: Building the 80/20 CP Matrix

At this phase, we are going to create a two-dimensional representation of how customers and products relate to each other in terms of revenue, as shown in figure 3. This is a simple but very important and effective phase of the 80/20 methodology. The physical representation of this matrix elicits a great number of findings. I highly recommend that the entire matrix be printed out and pasted on a large wall somewhere so the task force and management teams can have a live picture of the complexity handled by the business.

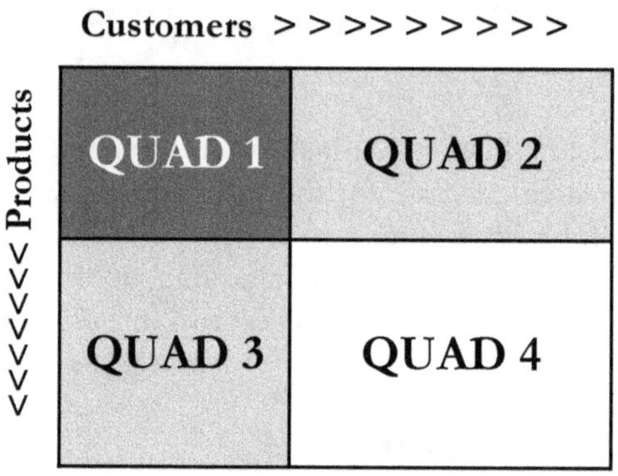

**Customers > > >> > > > > >**

Figure 3.

Customers (the x-axis) and products (the y-axis) are entered in descending order in the matrix. A vertical line is drawn at the cumulative 80 percent of revenue for customers and a horizontal line is drawn at the cumulative 80 percent of revenue for products. We then name each of the four quadrants: Q1, Q2, Q3 and Q4.

-Q1: contains high-volume customers buying high-volume products:
- HVC/HVP or 80/80.

-Q2: contains low-volume customers buying high-volume products:
- LVC/HVP or 80/20.

-Q3: contains high-volume customers buying low-volume products:
- HVC/LVP or 80/20.

-Q4: contains low-volume customers buying low-volume products:
- LVC/LVP or 20/20.

Using the data tables 4 and 5 plus the information contained in the database, created during the data-gathering phase, the next step is to create the complete 80/20 table.

## 80/20 customers and products (CP) Matrix:

CUSTOMERS

| PRODUCTS | A | B | C | D | E | F | G | ..... | K | L |
|---|---|---|---|---|---|---|---|---|---|---|
| 1 | 72.6 | 49.0 | | 48.4 | | | | | | |
| 2 | 149.2 | | 1.8 | 13.2 | | | | ..... | | |
| 3 | | 28.0 | 27.6 | | | 28.8 | | | 0.1 | 14.0 |
| 4 | 30.2 | 38.2 | | 11.9 | | | | ..... | | 0.3 |
| 5 | | | 35.5 | 40.8 | | | | | 0.1 | |
| 6 | | 54.4 | 21.7 | | | | | ..... | | |
| 7 | | | 26.7 | | | 0.2 | 15.0 | | 5.6 | |
| 8 | | | 18.8 | | 14.9 | | | ..... | | |
| 9 | | 16.9 | | 15.5 | | | | | | |
| 10 | | 17.9 | | | | | | ..... | | |
| 11 | | | | 5.2 | | | | | 8.4 | |
| 12 | | | 1.7 | | | | | ..... | 1.3 | |
| 13 | | | | | 0.1 | | 12.1 | | | |
| 14 | | | | | 9.2 | | | ..... | | |
| 15 | | | | | 6.6 | | | | | |
| 16 | 2.3 | | 1.8 | | | 1.7 | | ..... | | |
| 17 | | | 2.7 | | | 0.5 | | | 0.2 | |
| 18 | | | | | 1.3 | | 2.1 | ..... | | 0.1 |
| 19 | | | | | 0.6 | | | | | |
| 20 | | | | | | | | ..... | 0.3 | |
| **(Revenue $ x 1,000)** | $254.5 | $205.3 | $138.7 | $135.7 | $32.9 | $31.3 | $29.2 | ..... | $16.2 | $14.2 |
| | 27.3% | 49.4% | 64.3% | 78.9% | 82.5% | 85.8% | 89.0% | ..... | 98.5% | 100.0% |

| PRODUCTS | Revenue $ | Cum. % | Units | CM% |
|---|---|---|---|---|
| 1 | $170.1 | 18.3% | 12.2 | 28% |
| 2 | $164.3 | 35.9% | 9.1 | 26% |
| 3 | $129.6 | 49.9% | 8.6 | 32% |
| 4 | $81.1 | 58.6% | 6.8 | 25% |
| 5 | $80.7 | 67.3% | 4.7 | 23% |
| 6 | $76.2 | 75.4% | 4.2 | 26% |
| 7 | $70.9 | 83.1% | 3.9 | 18% |
| 8 | $33.9 | 86.7% | 2.3 | 35% |
| 9 | $32.5 | 90.2% | 2.3 | 32% |
| 10 | $17.9 | 92.1% | 1.2 | 32% |
| 11 | $13.7 | 93.6% | 1.0 | 28% |
| ........................ | | | | |
| 16 | $5.8 | 98.7% | 0.4 | 18% |
| 17 | $4.6 | 99.2% | 0.3 | 15% |
| 18 | $3.7 | 99.6% | 183 | 18% |
| 19 | $2.0 | 99.8% | 195 | 19% |
| 20 | $1.8 | 100.0% | 151 | 20% |

$930.5      61,455

Table 6.

The shades or colors in tables 4 and 5 are used to differentiate top, transitional, and bottom customers or products. They do not mean good, average, or bad. The same goes for the shades or colors used in the CP matrix represented in table 6. The matrix can be interpreted as a snapshot of the company's performance as it relates to these two datasets (customers and products interrelated by revenue) for the period of time selected. It is important to note that this is a dynamic situation and needs to be revised from time to time. In real examples, the matrix is likely to have a very large number of rows and columns, providing an excellent visualization of the complexity. Just by looking at the CP matrix, one can already observe unique patterns. They answer some questions and create new ones for the team.

✓ The relative size of the darker area (Q1 or 80/80) compared to the other quads reveals the following information and creates questions:

  -This area alone is responsible for making or breaking the business.
  -Are we devoting 80 percent of our resources and focus to Q1?

✓ The relative size of the clear or white area (Q4 or 20/20) compared to the other quads reveals the following information and creates questions:

  -Any effort put in this area is pulling away from what really matters.
  -Its size reveals a dimension of complexity.
  -How many transactions are supported in Q4?
  -Is Q4 getting the same (or more) amount of time and focus as Q1?
  -What is the real value of customers and products in Q4?

✓ The shape and size of the light gray areas (Q2 and Q3 or 80/20) reveals the following information and creates questions:

  -These are complementary areas that should only exist to support your "eighty" strategies.
  -How proliferated is your product line? Are your "eighty" customers buying these SKUs?
  -How complex is your customer base? How many transactions do they drive?
  -Are there any "strategic" customers that can be developed into Q1 customers?

-Are there any products that are low volume for us but high volume for the competition?

✓ The density and distribution in the matrix (blank versus populated cells) reveals the following information and creates questions:

-It is a measure of how well your product line is conceived for your segment.
-Are we making unique products for unique customers? How tailored or customized is our product offering?
-Do we have offerings that appeal to the entire customer base?

✓ The portfolio's completeness to "eighty" customers (population frequency) reveals the following information and creates questions:

-It shows if your vital customers are buying the entire line or only certain products.
-Do we have holes in our product line to major customers?
-Which customers are buying the entire line and which are not?
-Are our best customers buying our "eighty" products?

✓ The sales frequency of your products ("eighty" and "twenty") reveals the following information and creates questions:

-It depicts how well your products are distributed throughout the customer base.
-Are there "eighty" customers that do not buy your "eighty" products?
-Are the bulk of "twenty" products being sold to "eighty" customers?
-Are there gaps in your product portfolio for "eighty" customers?
-Are there obvious clusters of customers buying specific products?

A typical CP matrix distribution is shown on figure 4.

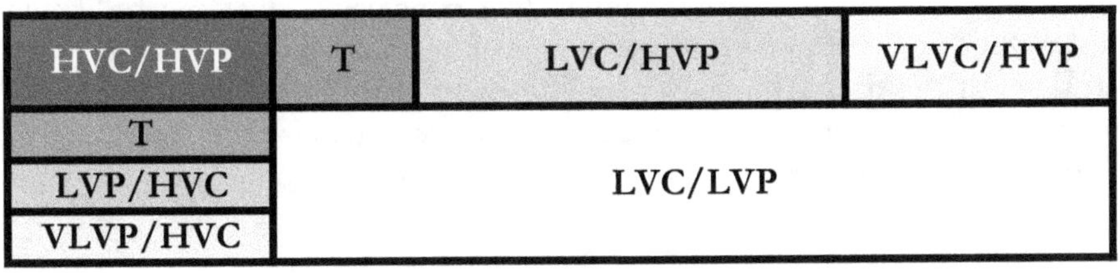

| HVC/HVP | T | LVC/HVP | VLVC/HVP |
|---|---|---|---|
| T<br>LVP/HVC<br>VLVP/HVC | LVC/LVP | | |

Figure 4.

45

In most cases, CP matrices present different data density by area, as shown in figure 4. We can classify the areas in the following way:

- -HVC/HVP: high-volume customers buying high volume products in quadrant 1. This is the "eighty" quadrant and we want to make it larger in relation to the other quadrants.
- -T: transitional areas as defined in tables 4 and 5. These are areas to monitor closely.
- -LVP/HVC: low-volume products being sold to high-volume customers. Suggests we need to carry these "twenty" products, but consider different strategies to create availability of the products and to charge for them.
- -LVC/HVP: low-volume customers buying high-volume products. These are the products we want the "twenty" customers to buy; however the support and attention we give these customers is less than what we should give to "eighty" customers.
- -VLVP/HVC: very-low-volume products being sold to high-volume customers: are these parts highly customized to "eighty" customers? If so, there is a good reason to charge more. Otherwise, these parts should be good candidates for product line simplification.
- -VLVC/HVP: very-low-volume customers buying high-volume products. Should you rechannel these customers to buy from other "eighty" customers?
- -LVC/LVP: low-volume customers buying low-volume products: should you be transacting in this quadrant at all? You need a strong reason to be here. This is the "twenty" of the "twenty". Probably there is more complexity associated with this quadrant than what you can recover from the market. This is the filter-out area.

## Step 4: Doing Quad Analysis

There are obviously many interesting conclusions that can be drawn from 80/20 CP matrices. Some are visual. Some require a little more analysis of the data. The denser the information in the database, the more you will want to drill down. Some questions will require the task force to look for more information to understand what is going on with your customer base.

A basic quad analysis requires simple calculations of the weight related to each quad in relation to revenue, volume, and contribution margins. An example, based on the dataset above, is shown on table 7.

**An example of quad analysis template (x 1,000):**

|  | Q1 | Q2 | Q3 | Q4 | Total |
|---|---|---|---|---|---|
| **# Parts** | 6 | 6 | 14 | 14 | 20 |
| % | 30% | 30% | 70% | 70% | |
| **Revenue $** | $623 | $79 | $111 | $117 | $931 |
| % | 67% | 8% | 12% | 13% | |
| **Units** | 34.8 | 5.2 | 7.3 | 8.5 | 55.8 |
| % | 57% | 9% | 12% | 14% | |
| **CM $ Total** | $166 | $25 | $31 | $27 | $248 |
| % | 67% | 10% | 12% | 11% | |
| **CM %** | 27% | 31% | 28% | 23% | 27% |

Table 7.

The pieces of information in each quadrant are as follows:

- # Parts: total number of items or different SKUs in each quadrant.
- Revenue $: total revenue dollars for the quadrant and percentage over total company's revenues.
- CM $ Total: contribution margin dollars for the quadrant and percentage over total company's contribution margin dollars.
- CM %: absolute contribution margin percentage for the quadrant.

Quad analysis makes it easier to understand the weight of each quadrant as it relates to revenue and contribution margin. It also starts giving you a sense of the complexity by looking at the distribution of units sold, mainly when it comes to Q4. In table 7, we can see that Q1 does not represent 80 percent of the revenues and margins (67% in this case). At the lowest contribution margin of all quads, 13 percent of the revenue is generated with low-volume customers buying low-volume parts in Q4. This alone is a sign that the company is not being remunerated adequately for complexity, since the margins should be a lot higher in this quad.

But how do we compare the outcome of the analysis? Is there a golden ratio among the quads? It really depends on the type of business you are in. There are no packaged answers, only common sense. In general, the strategy is to accomplish the following targets:

✓ Maximize Q1 revenue and grow profitably:
  -Get as close to 80 percent of the total revenue as possible.
✓ Manage Q2 and Q3 to help support growth of Q1:
  -Around 15 percent of combined revenues.
✓ Minimize Q4 to reduce complexity:
  -No more than 5 percent of total revenues.

In table 7, if we were to apply the targets above, you would see an expansion of Q1 by more than 10 percent, a small reduction in Q2 and Q3 of about 5 percent, and a larger reduction of Q4 by 8 percent. Table 8 below shows the gaps for each quadrant.

| Quadrant | Revenue $ | Actual % | "Target" % | Gap % |
|---|---|---|---|---|
| Q1 | $623 | 67% | 80% | +13% |
| Q2/Q3 | $190 | 20% | 15% | -5% |
| Q4 | $117 | 13% | 5% | -8% |
| Total | $930 | 100% | 100% | |

Table 8.

After optimizing the matrix and reaching these targets, the CP matrix can look very different, as seen in figure 5.

**Original (pre-optimization) customer product matrix:**

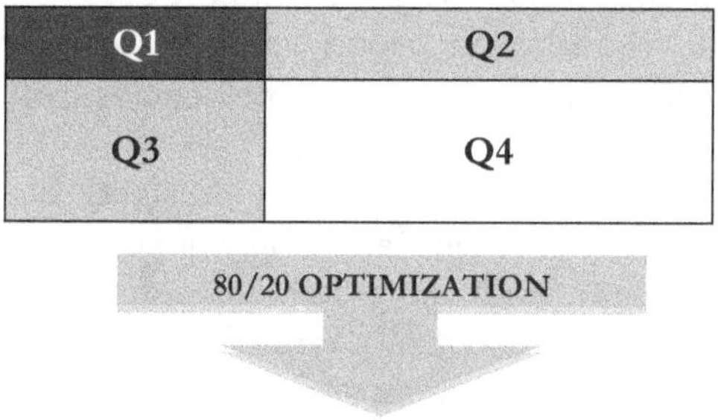

**Refocused (post-optimization) customer product matrix:**

Figure 5.

Other examples of analyses or metrics that can be used to further refine or to reach new conclusions are listed in table 9.

| ANALYSES / METRICS | HOW TO MEASURE? | WHAT IS TELLS YOU? |
|---|---|---|
| Sales density | The number of cells containing sales revenues versus the total number of cells per quadrant. | Reveals the completeness of a product portfolio or the existence of too many gaps. |
| Customer adherence | The percentage of SKUs available to be bought by each customer. | Reveals whether customers are buying the entire portfolio or are cherry-picking. |
| Transaction complexity | The number of units sold per invoice per quadrant. | Shows the level of interaction required to get the sale. |
| Special products | The number of sales invoices by product across the entire customer base. | Shows whether a product is being bought by only a few customers. |
| Low-profitability products | The products selling below a certain margin threshold. | Reveals the SKUs that need to be improved, from a margin stand-point. |
| Low-profitability customers | The overall customer margin below a certain threshold. | Points to improvement actions, depending on whether customers are "eighty" or "twenty". |
| Different segmentation | The CP matrix redone for different market segments within the "eighty". | Shows whether the company is underperforming in a specific market segment. |
| Unit volume matrix | Use unit volume instead of revenues to do the CP matrix. | Gives an idea about volume distribution and points to freight cost. |
| Turns and earns | The contribution margin percentage multiplied by units. | Shows the relative value of earnings power by customer and by SKU. |
| Transactions per customer | Number of invoices per customer. | Gives an idea about the service level required by a customer. |

Table 9.

## Step 5: Developing Optimization Strategies

Several iterations of the matrix and supplementary analyses may be necessary until the data talks. Once it does, you can start making progress right away, by taking actions that will improve the overall performance. The goal here is to focus on what can be done with customers and products in the short-term to improve profitability and to reduce complexity. The four quads have their own mantras when it comes to optimization and growth in each one.

| YES, MAKE IT BETTER | YES, BUT |
|---|---|
| YES, BUT | ARE WE SURE? |

Figure 6.

# Optimize Q1

Not all customers are equal; some customers are more equal than others. The mantra for Q1 is Yes, Make It Better. Q1 is the most important of all quadrants—the center of gravity of the business. This is where substantial energy and focus should be applied first. It should take priority over fixing other quadrants.

1.  Know everything there is to know about the "eighty" customers.

    Understand the market segment in-depth—its trends, threats, and opportunities. Find out who the competition is and who their "eighty" customers are. Walk in your customers' shoes to understand their pain points and needs, and involve them in your product innovation efforts. Explore in detail the customers' statuses at every business review meeting.

2.  Create a different commercial approach for dealing with the "eighty" customers.

Make it simple for the "eighty" customers to do business with you. Create a unique and better way for these customers to interact with your company, and make them feel special. Simplify the ordering approach, from telephone hotlines and special Internet portals to dedicated sales and relationship management people.

**Separate high- and low-volume customers:**

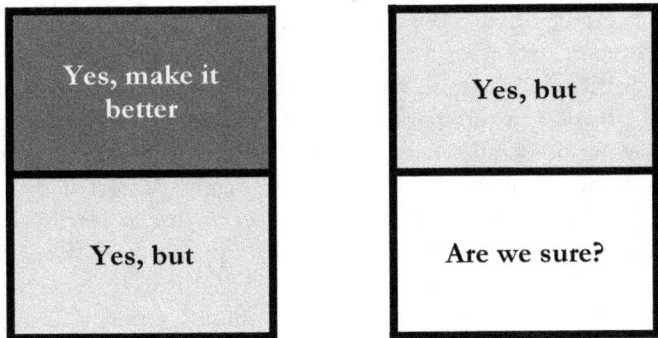

Figure 7.

3.  Go "mining" to find and develop more "eighty" customers.

Are there "twenty" customers in your matrix today that should be developed into the "eighty"? What about your competition's "eighty" customers? Once you know the vital customers and products, it will be easier to better define the target segment for acquiring new ones. Bear in mind it can be more effective to find the next million dollars in sales from within the existing customer base than to look for new customers. In reality, this is the thinking behind segmentation and specialization— to find niches that you can focus on and grow in within the existing "eighty." That brings us to the next strategy.

4.  Look for subsegment(s) in the existing customer base.

Are there market niches within the segment that need attention? Does it make sense to consider segmenting the customer base into two or more commercial BUs? By creating one or more subsegments within the "eighty," you can assign focused champions to dive deep into the specific needs of these customers and the fractal markets. Once you recut the matrix based on the new segmentation approach, some of the old "twenty" customers will become part of the new "eighty." Later on, if successful, these segments tend to evolve into full-fledged BUs with their own dedicated resources. If they are not successful in growing, they tend to de-segment and go back to the original approach. But nothing or very little is lost in this expedition for new segments, only gains and new insights into the "eighty."

5.   Improve the competitiveness of your "eighty" products.

Any contribution margin enhancement in Q1 has an incredibly positive effect on the overall gross margin of the company. A small improvement here goes a long way toward your goal. In order to boost your contribution margin, you need to understand how to impact your pricing position in the market (if possible) and your variable cost. Start by knowing in detail where your prices and portfolio offerings stand versus your competitor's. Does your "eighty" portfolio match the "eighty" of the market? How do you compare in terms of features, benefits, and prices? Is there an obvious opportunity? In most cases, it is not possible to increase prices in Q1 right away. You will need a margin enhancement and an effective sourcing strategy to improve the profitability.

This is where you should apply the best resources to make Q1 better. Cost reduction is not only a one-time effort but also an ongoing imperative. Many tools exist including frequent teardown workshops with competitive products and value engineering sessions. Involve your best customers if you can. Try to optimize direct materials (new sources and product changes) and improve manufacturing processes. Dedicate your best high-volume production lines (in-lines) to make the "eighty" products. Automate the production process as much as you can.

6.   Measure the financial performance of the "eighty" differently.

Use direct costing methods to track the contribution margins for the "eighty" (see chapter 5.4 on direct costing). You need to know the true profitability picture of the "eighty" (both individual products and customers) and not use data that is polluted with estimated cost figures. Track net performance (net of inflation) productivity for materials, labor, and other variable expenses necessary to produce the "eighty" products. Refresh the customers and products (CP) matrix and quad analysis recurrently.

## Minimize Q4

Why work on Q4 before working on Q2 and Q3? Simply because Q4 is easier to deal with compared with the other quads. On top of that, Q4 is a nuisance. You will be reducing "noise" that can interfere with the key work. But no matter how hard you work here, it won't move the needle too much, so don't waste a lot of time. Move quickly and decisively and then go on to improve Q2 and Q3. Although its existence is almost unavoidable, you need a very good reason to have a lot of revenue tied to this quadrant. This is why the mantra here is Are You Sure?

7.   Increase prices for products with below average margins right away.

The most effective way to shrink Q4 quickly is to raise prices immediately. Believe me, you are not going to hurt anything. If you are going to have any revenues in this quad, you need to be adequately compensated for dealing with complexity. Contribution margins need to be significantly higher than in other quads, mainly because you may not be sure how accurate your margins are in this quad. So give yourself a safety margin. For example, if your overall CM on Q1 is 30 percent, then your target should be a minimum of 45 percent or more in Q4. The best approach is to raise prices across the board, especially for those SKUs that are primarily sold to "twenty" customers, and then correct distortions in the low-volume products, either by pricing up SKUs that fall below a certain threshold (30 percent margin is a good start in our example) or by simply eliminating very low-volume SKUs.

Let the market laws deal with this quad. Some customers will walk away, and that may be a good thing. In my experience, the majority of the customers will stay and pay the higher price. There are reasons why they are buying here, and pricing is probably not the first one. In most cases, they are looking for availability and recognizing that it is more efficient to deal with a limited number of suppliers. You are doing the hard job for them, so there is nothing wrong with getting paid more for the service. At the end, my experience also tells me that the margins will improve and the optimization will take its course naturally, without having to "fire" or re-channel (many) customers.

8.   Don't allow further growth in Q4 by filtering out new entrants.

Raising prices is the most effective way to improve Q4, but phasing out the bottom of your low-volume products may also be necessary, especially products that have very little margin and products that are not being sold to "eighty" customers. The majority of product and customer issues will be dealt in Q2 and Q3, so here you only deal with the obvious problems. The key point is to stop the sales and engineering teams from creating more activity in Q4. The screening process to avoid enlargement of Q4 should be simple enough that sales people know the rules before they attempt to create a sale in this quad. I will discuss filtering when I cover Q3 and Q4 and when I talk about product line simplification.

## Optimize Q2 and Q3

The mantra for Q2 and Q3 is Yes, But. You know and admit that you will have to do business in these quads, but you want to be very selective and manage these two quadrants actively. You do not want to allow complexity to creep in. When I discuss product line simplification (PLS), I will be largely addressing the optimization of Q3. When I talk about segmentation, I will tackle issues from Q2. However, there are also many short-term benefits that be obtained this early in the process by observing some basic rules.

9.  Decide whether there are any future "eighty" customers.

On the border of Q1, towards the low-volume customers, there are transitional customers to be examined carefully. We normally find many customers to be growable or strategic among the "twenty." These are target customers that are in our "twenty" today, but are considered "eighty" in the market, for example. Other customers have the potential to grow significantly in their markets or geography (sleeper customers). The definition of strategic or sleeper vary by business, but there are multiple reasons why we want to identify and target these customers for bringing them into the "eighty." At the same time, as previously discussed, when you segment the matrix differently, you will find that some of the original "twenty" customers are already migrating into the new segmented "eighty." This is to be expected and exploited.

10. Differentiate terms and conditions between "eighty" and "twenty" customers.

I already made this point when I talked about differentiating the commercial conditions in relation to "eighty" customers. When it comes to the "twenty" customers (excluding the transitional ones and the future "eighty" ones), the goal is to reduce the business's internal complexity and allow the market laws to take their natural courses. Many approaches are used here, such as increasing delivery times (reducing the company's inventory needs), charging (or charging more) for shipments, asking for different payment terms and conditions, requiring minimum order quantities, creating longer purchasing forecasts, and so on. The idea is to expand the service gap between the vital few and the trivial many while making the complexity transparent for the low-volume customers. As with Q4, experience will show that a large majority of customers will continue to buy from the company even with these changes.

11. Analyze transactions and earning power by customer by SKU.

Before we start reducing portfolio complexity, it is important to understand the absolute contribution from each SKU and compare that with a metric that provides an idea about the level of complexity of carrying that SKU. One useful indicator is the number of transactions generated by each SKU, for example in the form of units per invoice. To perform this analysis, you recast the CP matrix in terms of total contribution margin dollars (CM multiplied by units) by customer and by SKU. You can then list on the edges of the CP Matrix the ratio of units per invoice for each SKU, as well as the ratio of units per invoice for each customer. I've also seen the 80/20 matrices redone in terms of contribution margin dollars per invoice by customer and by SKU. The important point is to find the metrics that work best for your type of business or situation.

12. Simplify the product portfolio.

Later on I will cover a broader initiative for systematic product line simplification (PLS). At this point, similar to what was done in Q4, we can resort to picking the low-hanging fruit to alleviate major distortions that exist. Setting an overall contribution margin target for Q3 is always a good start, and here again it should be higher than that of Q1 (normally by 5 to 10 points). Since we are not doing PLS here yet, we will be selective about our target population by excluding the following: (1) the "eighty" and the transitional products from the CP matrix, (2) the "eighty" products from the turns and earns matrix (a different version of the CP matrix as explained in table 6, and (3) those SKUs that present a contribution margin above an established margin threshold. On the other hand, the prime targets will be: (1) those "twenty" products at the bottom of the matrix that sell very infrequently, (2) the "twenty" products below the margin threshold, and (3) the "twenty" SKUs with the lowest turns and earns.

13. Create special availability for the "twenty" products.

I've talked about the necessity to dedicate the most productive and effective resources to make the "eighty" available at the lowest possible cost and to work with an accurate contribution margin. We will also cover these strategies in more detail later in this book. On the other hand, the low-volume products need a differentiated sourcing strategy to accomplish the following goals: (1) prevent the complexity of the "twenty" from contaminating the "eighty," (2) minimize the requirement for additional working capital and inventory (low turns and earns), and (3) allow for a more accurate cost picture. The basic strategy here is physical separation between "eighty" and "twenty."

**High- and low-volume product separation:**

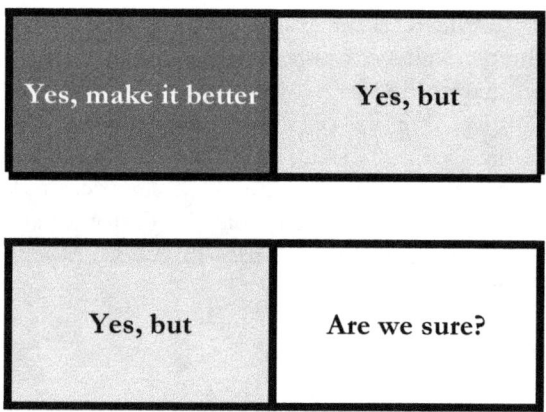

Figure 8.

There are short-term optimization actions that can be adopted without sacrificing the internal physical separation strategies between high- and low-volume products, which will be discussed later in this book. They range from carrying a little inventory using MRD (market rate of demand) all the way to completely outsourcing production of the low-volume SKUs, which are in most cases at the tail of the demand curve. Companies usually resist outsourcing for different reasons, but their resistance is mainly due to the fact that "twenty" production is entangled with "eighty" production, distorting the variable cost information. If the outsourcing analysis is done on only a variable cost basis, it becomes hard to find a supplier that can offer a low enough cost to beat the internal variable margin. Outsourcing at this stage requires a leap of faith, knowing that you will not only be replacing the variable cost with a fixed price, but you will also be reducing complexity (or hidden variable and indirect cost). But then again, we are talking about the "twenty," where knowing the true cost (to reflect in the price) is more important than trying to reduce the cost. The effort to reduce cost is not necessarily worthy here when compared to the benefits of raising prices and allowing the price-elasticity law to take effect.

14. Filter customers and products and re-channel some low-volume customers.

One of the myths around 80/20 is the idea that you have to "fire" low-volume customers. I can attest from experience this is hardly the case. The most effective way to reduce complexity in the customer base is to allow the pricing and portfolio optimization strategies above to do their jobs. Rechanneling customers or redirecting their orders to other high-volume customers are used as a way to simplify and strengthen the relationships with "eighty" customers. At the end, after applying these strategies, the company only needs to develop clear rules and educate its employees on how to avoid creating more complexity.

Table 10 shows the summary of the 14 most used optimization strategies for the CP matrix, divided by quadrant.

| OPTIMIZATION STRATEGIES | |
|---|---|
| **Optimize Q1<br>(HVC buying HVP)** | |
| 1 | Know everything there is to know about the "eighty" customers. |
| 2 | Create a different approach for dealing with the "eighty" customers. |
| 3 | Go "mining" to find and develop more "eighty" customers. |
| 4 | Look for subsegment(s) in the existing customer base. |
| 5 | Improve the competitiveness of your "eighty" products. |
| 6 | Measure the financial performance of the "eighty" differently. |
| **Minimize Q4<br>(LVC buying LVP)** | |
| 7 | Increase prices for products with below average margins right away. |
| 8 | Don't allow further growth in Q4 by filtering out new entrants. |
| **Optimize Q2 and Q3<br>(LVC buying HVP and HVC buying LVP)** | |
| 9 | Decide whether there are any future "eighty" customers. |
| 10 | Differentiate terms and conditions between "eighty" and "twenty" customers. |
| 11 | Analyze transactions and earning power by customer by SKU. |
| 12 | Simplify the product portfolio. |
| 13 | Create special availability for the "twenty" products. |
| 14 | Filter customers and products and re-channel some low-volume customers. |

Table 10.

## Step 6: Planning for Next Phases

After the data talks, then it's time to act. You will probably have a list of actions originating from the optimization ideas above, and you can start executing them right away. As you start seeing progress from these actions, you will want to move into what I call the physical parts of 80/20, such as the separation of high- and low-volume parts at the production line, the simplification of complex business processes, and the streamlining of your product portfolio. You may even be able to contemplate the focus (F) part of the ASFG cycle that deals with the segmentation of the business, as the data jumps at you with more obvious segmentation ideas.

Here again is where 80/20 critical thinking needs to be applied to determine what will give you the best results. There is no rigid formula for deciding what to do next, but before you jump at the hard pruning and segmentation, I've always found it extremely useful to do a dry run of new approaches using the existing business structure, with the difference that you create new and expanded focus areas with additional leadership sharing the same resources for a while. For example, if you have thought of a new market segmentation approach during the analytics phase, you may want to segment the sales teams at first and experiment with that concept before fully segmenting the BUs.

The key here is to allow the outcome of every new phase to lead you into the next one, as long as you stay loyal to the implementation cycle and to 80/20 thinking. But do refresh the analytics as you go since they change often, especially after you start the optimization process. They will continue to guide the work at all subsequent phases of 80/20.

## Case Example: CP Matrix of a Brake Parts Manufacturer for Heavy-Duty Vehicles

This company is a manufacturer of air brakes and air brake parts for trucks, buses, and trailers. It serves both OEMs (original equipment manufacturers) and aftermarket customers (independent parts retailers and OEM service organizations). The company decided to embrace 80/20 starting with the aftermarket BU. The implementation team created the CP matrix using revenue, volume, and margin data from the previous twelve months.

## Actions to Take After the Quad Analysis

I recommend the following actions for Q1:

-Establish Q1 overall contribution margin goal of 30 percent to reach double-digit return on sales.

-Perform root cause analysis to discover why some SKUs are below the threshold or even show negative margin, and decide what to do. Look at the market landscape and competitors for those items. Are you selling below market price? Do you have a comparable specification to the competition? Can you learn anything from your competitor's products? Conduct value engineering analysis on most valuable SKUs.

-Look at the customers in Q1 and decide whether they are buying your entire offering or whether they are buying only specific products.

-Look at the total contribution margin from each of your "eighty" customers.

I recommend the following actions for Q4:

-Establish the minimum contribution margin that you should have in this quad (in this case, 45 percent).

-Look at the current overall margin, and raise the prices across the board in Q4 to meet your target. Don't worry about raising prices for all products —just provide a significant price increase.

I recommend the following actions for Q2:

-Look at each customer to decide whether there are strategic customers in the mix that you want to develop into "eighty" customers. Are these customers currently in the "eighty" of your competitor's matrix? What do you have to do to bring them into your "eighty"?

-Look at transitional customers and see where they are as far as total contribution margins and buying your entire portfolio. Can you do anything to improve margins?

-Decide which customers will be rechanneled to your "eighty" customers.

I recommend the following actions for Q3:

-Draw a line to define the transitional area, the low-volume products, and the very low-volume products, using the information on tables 4 and 5. Are there very low-volume products that you should simply drop from your portfolio? Find out the total contribution margin for each of these three areas of the matrix.

-Define a contribution margin target for Q3 (in this case, 35 percent). Identify those transitional SKUs that are below the target margin. Define a plan for each SKU you identify (similar to Q1).

-Are there SKUs in your "twenty" that are "eighty" for the market? Do you have a competitive issue? What is the root cause for each one?
-Look at the low-volume products and decide which ones or which product families are best candidates for outsourcing. Should you adopt different inventory-keeping policies?

-Increase prices in the low-volume section to meet the overall target margin right away.

As preparation for the next phases of the 80/20 BPI, the company decided to work on different views of the CP matrix by breaking the aftermarket into two segments based on the experience of the sales and marketing people:

-By channel: independent aftermarket (IAM) and OEM service (OES).
-By application—truck and trailer (T&T) and bus (Bus).

The two matrices have shown very different characteristics, and based on further competitive analysis, the company was able to conclude that the OES channel was underdeveloped. These further analytics led them to establish two commercial divisions within the aftermarket BU. Each division was led by a general manager, who held the overall responsibility for improving their CP matrix in terms of growth, contribution margin, customer development, and product portfolio. The OES division grew quickly with the newly acquired focus, and after only one year, they could see meaningful transformation (clearly shown in the CP matrix). At this point, the company decided to split the aftermarket into two distinct BUs—IAM (independent aftermarket) and OES (OEM service). Each business was led by its respective general manager (GM) and had its own people and warehouses to store parts. The GMs had clear profit and loss (P&L) accountability.

Over time, these businesses grew faster and specialized their products, sales approaches, services, and logistics to fit their new respective markets. The additional overhead added to OES segment to provide the needed structure was quickly offset by the growth in terms of new revenues and return on sales (ROS) growth. The overall contribution margins improved, and the CP matrices were optimized significantly. Eventually, each business unit developed new products and capabilities, and the IAM BU ventured into an acquisition of another aftermarket company. After a couple of years, the IAM BU performed the entire 80/20 process over and decided to segment itself again, this time based on truck and trailer (T&T), and bus (Bus) applications.

# CHAPTER 5
# COMPLEXITY REDUCTION

*It seems that perfection is reached, not when there is nothing left to add, but when there is nothing left to take away.*

*—Antoine de Saint Exupéry*

How many times have you heard a successful entrepreneur say that a business idea was conceived on a paper napkin at a restaurant? In fact, if you look around, you may find paper napkins framed and hanging on office walls of a few companies. The proud entrepreneur can hardly remember what it was like to run the business when it was just a simple, single-minded enterprise propelled by the power of a distinct idea and purpose. Something happened that created a lot of complexity and activity that is not necessarily aligned with the original vision.

Almost every business starts simple and becomes complex as it grows and develops. As scale changes, simplicity gives way to layers of structure and chaos. When complexity creeps in without control and is not properly managed, it can push against value creation and profitability. In reality, the problem is not extra scale but extra complexity. Additional scale, without additional complexity, will always give lower costs. But most of the time when a business grows, we provide more services and products, therefore increasing complexity and cost.

The complexity of the product portfolio can be a hindrance to customer service levels, profitability and growth. Without product line simplification focus, non-value-added complexity will prevail over time.

Eliminating this can have huge impact on profits and growth. When the product offering of a company contains just a small amount of variation, the impact of adding new offerings is relatively minor. However, as this complexity grows in the form of low-volume products and customers, just a few additional products can create a disproportional increase in complexity costs.

Compounding the issue of product and service portfolio proliferation are other complications arising from multiple organizational changes and structural mitosis. The constant swing of the pendulum to accommodate opposing leadership styles, multiple attempts to centralize or disperse shared resources, and the frequent reengineering of core processes ends up creating a lot of extra complexity. And then there is the important issue of managerial habits, since managers often behave in ways that make the problem worse.

At the root of all this is the unfailing ability that human beings have to complicate things for themselves and for others. In today's convoluted business world, leaders do not always make it simple and keep it simple. Managers are human beings, and they are also educated to expect and embrace complexity. It can be intellectually stimulating and sometimes offers job security. Managers work harder (not necessarily smarter) to cover all the bases and strive to excel on too many fronts. Unless firms are facing an economic crisis or have exceptional leaders who push for simplicity, excessive management activity is virtually guaranteed.

We find that managers often ignore or rarely take advantage of the natural imbalances that exist in business. They don't use 80/20 thinking to simplify life for their subordinates. They tend to average all inputs and equalize their efforts across people, decisions, and data, becoming victims of the perverse side of the 80/20 rule. They frequently forget to be selective. A simple request for information, for example, can lead to the creation of a number of new reports and unnecessary activities.

Hubert Crowell describes the complexity issue very nicely:

*"Businesses become unprofitable because they accept complexity and dedicate resources and overhead to too many unprofitable activities. Very profitable businesses do not require as much overhead. Ideally a business could be solely composed of value-added activities, making the same or more profit, provided that things are organized differently. Understanding the cost of complexity allows us to take a major leap forward in the debate about*

*corporate size. It is not that small is beautiful. All other things being equal, big is beautiful. But all other things are not equal. Big is only ugly and expensive because it is complex. Big can be beautiful. But it is simplicity that is always beautiful.'*[xxii]

*'What is most simple and standardized is hugely more productive and cost-effective than what is complicated. Managers should always try to identify the simplest 20 percent of any product range, process, marketing message, sales channel, product design, product-manufacturing process, service delivery, or customer feedback mechanism. Refine the simplest 20 percent until it is as simple as you can make it. Make the simplest 20 percent as high quality and consistent as imaginable. Whenever something has become complex, simplify it; if you cannot, then eliminate it.'*[xxiii]

Sometimes there is a genuine need for variety and customization of services and products. However, if there needs to be complexity because customers demand and pay for it, complexity itself needs to be made simple and turned into a system of building blocks or a LEGO©-like system. There has to be economic value associated with complexity, and your business model should be able to capture the value when a customer wants something unique. If not, then customization becomes a mere obstacle for value creation and can be the single biggest reason for low profitability, mediocre customer service, and lack of growth. Without 80/20 thinking, or in the absence of deliberate focus to avoid non-value-added activities, complexity will inevitably grow beyond control and create tough problems for managers.

One prime example of managed complexity that creates customer value and sustained profitability is Scania, the global Swedish truck maker. Scania is the premium truck manufacturer in the world. It prides itself on a modular system that provides customers with multiple options and configurations. At the same time, their engineering offices and plants are simple: they use a limited number of building blocks with many variations. Scania products share components across a wide range of vehicles and applications. For example, all of Scania's truck cabs—regardless of size— have the same interface with the chassis. All engines and gearboxes have the same mounting points on the chassis, irrespective of size. The chassis in turn is built up by a large number of frame components that fit together in innumerable combinations. Scania laid the groundwork for modularization more than fifty years ago and has been refining the system ever since.

If properly managed to create customer value, as Scania does, variety and customization can be a source of competitive advantage for the business. Customers can have an exceptionally broad number of options that enable products to be tailored to any specific need. Good complexity should be directed toward simplifying life for customers, not toward making your life miserable. The flip side is also true. When not actively managed, complexity can creep in and destroy value, making the customer's life miserable. The best approach is not to allow complexity to creep in in the first place. Once it does, the question becomes how to stop it from growing and how to reduce it. Even the process of managing and measuring complexity must be simplified.

Our world is growing more and more complex every day. We have many driving forces adding to this complexity and very few creating simplicity. Companies like Dell, Scania, and IKEA, where "simplicity is a virtue", are very rare. In his new book *Managing Complexity in our Organizations*, Ulrich Steger at IMD Business School in Lausanne tells us a lot about how complexity is still driving us away from useful simplicity. "Standardization of core processes is important when reducing complexity. There are diverse systems within companies that are often incompatible and resemble patchworks of undisciplined, IT-enabled business processes and redundant databases. The information itself is often quite diverse and is an important complexity driver."[xxiv]

The 80/20 methodology has its own taxonomy and its own information-modeling approach that uses simple analytics. The simple 80/20 tools help create simplicity and represent the best approach to understand which resources are truly earning a premium versus those that are mostly inducing systemic cost into the company. The analytics point to where simplicity needs to be created in the product portfolio and helps develop a model of sustainable growth and profitability.

Beyond product complexity, attacking all other complexity dimensions with simplification strategies is a necessity to maintain profitable growth. Simplifying requires deliberate management focus and diligence to execute. Throughout the entire 80/20 BPI cycle, you will notice strong emphasis toward such strategies to tackle multiple drivers of complexity, as shown in table 11.

**Complexity drivers and simplification methods:**

| COMPLEXITY DIMENSION TO ATTACK | 80/20 BPI METHOD TO USE | EXPECTED RESULT |
|---|---|---|
| Organizational structure | Market segment-focused BUs | Significantly reduced overhead costs and increased profitability. |
| Transaction complexity | Optimization using CP matrix | Reduced number of transactions and less management complexity. |
| Product portfolio | Product line simplification (PLS) | Reduction in portfolio complexity and product complexity management. |
| Business processes | Business process simplification (BPS) | Increased process efficiency and lowered automation costs. |
| Sourcing and manufacturing | Product availability simplification (PAS) | Increased contribution margins and lowered overhead costs. |
| Accounting and key performance indicators (KPIs) | Lean metrics | Simpler, more accurate, real-time information. |
| Managerial habits | 80/20 thinking | Higher focus on productivity and business scale-ability. |

Table 11.

Table 11 above shows the main complexity dimensions and the equivalent tools to introduce simplicity. In the specific simplification phase of the 80/20 BPI implementation cycle, I will detail the following tools:

1.  Product line simplification (PLS) reduces complexity in the existing product or service portfolio and creates filters to ensure that only desirable or good complexity enters the company.

2.  Business process simplification (BPS) simplifies and streamlines administrative processes, making changes that will result in greater efficiency and productivity. It should be used not only when complexity is present but also before any IT-based automation is introduced.

3.  Product availability simplification (PAS) simplifies and improves the way products or services are made available to customers under the 80/20 BPI. It starts with analytics and goes through the available physical separation methods to increase the focus on and reduce the costs of the "eighty" products.

4.  Finance and accounting simplification (lean metrics) covers not only the most important metrics used to run a business based on the 80/20 BPI, such as contribution margin and productivity, but it also proposes a change to the way we look at costs and financial metrics versus traditional methods.

I recommended that PLS, PAS, and lean metrics be executed in this order following the analytics and optimization phases. BPS can be implemented at any time during the simplification phase or during any other phase of the 80/20 BPI implementation cycle. This sequence is important, since the product offering needs to be simplified before a sourcing strategy and a manufacturing plan can be developed. The metrics will then be established to track the optimized stage of sourcing and production. On the other hand, business processes are normally not dependent on prior simplification steps in order to be improved. I will now go into each of the simplification tools above in more detail, starting with product line simplification (PLS).

## CHAPTER 5.1
## PRODUCT LINE SIMPLIFICATION (PLS)

*Profits are proportional to revenues; costs are proportional to transactions and to the number of discrete products.*

PLS is a methodology created to improve the profitability of businesses by simplifying product offerings while improving customer satisfaction and optimizing the price-benefit equation. It aligns manufacturing processes to support the product line while defining a clear position on how special offers will be made available and to whom. As a result, sales volumes increase, and production costs decrease. PLS reduces the number of discrete products, consistent with the business strategy. It makes all products pass the acid test, which asks why a product is offered and to whom. A product offering that is simple and well designed can be produced and delivered in a cost-effective, efficient, and consistent manner. Other benefits from simplification include the following:

-Improved competitiveness
-Better contribution margins
-Higher market share with better prices
-Less complexity to manage the business
-Improved customer service and product availability

Complexity in the product line reveals itself in obvious ways, such as in too many products and too many customers. Other visible signs of complexity are too many part numbers and too many suppliers and transactions. But there are some less apparent issues driven by product line complexity, such as too many systems, too many reports, too many procedures, and last but not least, too many people creating and maintaining SKUs. The top symptoms of elevated complexity are shown in table 12.

| SIMPTOMS OF ELEVATED COMPLEXITY (PAIN INDEX) | |
|---|---|
| 1 | Poor shipping performance (late and incomplete). |
| 2 | A typical pattern shows in the 80/20 CP matrix—20 percent of the products account for over 80 percent of the sales. |
| 3 | A significant number of products have minimal sales, and there is slow and obsolete inventory of such items. |
| 4 | More than seventy percent of product designs are made for similar applications, but sold to different customers. |
| 5 | Numerous subtle design variations in similar parts. |
| 6 | Number of new parts increases daily with little or no discussion. |
| 7 | Tailored parts interfere with standard products. |

Table 12.

PLS needs to be executed with an intense focus on product design and product cost. It starts with 80/20 analytics and is conducted using some of the same methods and tools used by teams in innovation workshops to generate new ideas. A few of these ideation methods will be explained in chapter 7, the innovation section of this book. PLS requires a disciplined process for design optimization and sometimes needs creative thinking to come up with product line architectures that build on each other, as offered by Scania. PLS is not a mere exercise to eliminate entire sections of the portfolio or even to purge low-volume part numbers. PLS is a tool designed to align the needs of the customer with the needs of the company.

Successful product line simplification is customer-centric and capable of identifying products or features that will satisfy application needs and address market pain points, as opposed to just offering a variety of designs to choose from. PLS cannot be driven by manufacturing, engineering, or purchasing in isolation from other areas. It needs to be a collaborative and multidisciplinary effort by different areas of the business with an eye on the customer application. PLS takes time and effort and is not an overnight exercise.

Table 13 below explain when and how to best use PLS, in order to avoid common application mistakes.

| APPLY PLS TO | DO NOT APPLY PLS IF |
|---|---|
| Reduce parts-count or the number of discrete products within a product portfolio, consistent with your business strategy. | You are just aiming to eliminate low-volume part numbers. |
| Create a filter to decide: why do we have to offer the product and to whom? | Your intent is to completely eliminate a business line. |
| Define a clear position on tailored products: who should get them and how they are to be priced and produced? | You are going to leave customers without viable options to satisfy their applications needs. |
| Align manufacturing processes to support the product line. | It is being driven by manufacturing in isolation from other parts of the business. |
| Couple the effort with the overall margin improvement work. | You believe this is an over-night exercise, since it takes time and effort. |

Table 13.

Reducing complexity in the product or service portfolio is accomplished by applying a combination of three processes: (1) pricing for customization, (2) product line optimization, and (3) new product introduction screening.

Pricing for customization is primarily executed at the analytics and optimization phase of the 80/20 methodology, since we needed to account for combined customer- and market-segment dynamics. The PLS tool will primarily focus on two fronts—product line optimization and new product screening. Both actions are driven from inside the organization by a dedicated team or task force. The primary focus of PLS is on the reduction of part numbers or SKUs.

The importance of reducing part numbers and SKUs can not be underestimated, as described in this paragraph from the outstanding AME article "The Spirit in the Walls: A Pattern for High Performance at Scania":

*"Everyone believes that a manufacturer will improve costs and profitability by reducing the number of different parts in its products. And for good reason. With fewer different parts, less effort and resources are required to design, make, and service a product line. Accordingly, activity-based cost management*

*systems routinely use part-number count as a cost driver to estimate how much financial performance will improve by reducing the number of different parts. However, it is not well understood that cost-driver information may capture only a small fraction of the financial improvement that part-number austerity makes possible.'*[xxv]

The task force should be formed from within the BU with people from sales, marketing, manufacturing, engineering, and accounting. They must have direct decision-making authority. The work steps and actions to be taken are shown in table 14.

| | STEPS | ACTIONS |
|---|---|---|
| 1 | Develop the 80/20 CP matrix analytics | -Study 80/20 analytics<br>-Find sales revenues and margins<br>-Do market segment analysis<br>-Identify high- and low- volume products |
| 2 | Study the need for PLS with the team members | -Identify complexity |
| 3 | Define the PLS plan for the BU | -Set objectives |
| 4 | Set the goals and objectives for PLS plan | -Decide vision |
| 5 | Deal with organizational obstacles and PLS myths | -Communicate broadly |
| 6 | Train the personnel to understand PLS | -Train |
| 7 | Explain to the organization PLS relationship with productivity and service | -Sell |
| 8 | Develop the project plan | -Plan |
| 9 | Start implementation | -Drop marginal products<br>-Price up low-volume<br>-Redesign the product<br>-Develop outsourcing plan<br>-Separate manufacturing<br>-Control admissions and deletions of new products |
| 10 | Measure and review often | -Measure |

Table 14.

The initial focus of PLS should only be whether a product or an item will be included in the product offering or not. Leave the make or buy decisions for later. There is an entire section devoted to outsourcing decisions in the product availability simplification chapter. At the beginning of the PLS process, it is a lot more important to decide what to drop and what to include. The decision to include a product is primarily made by the commercial people in support of marketing strategies, market pain points, and end user needs.

Focus on high-volume "eighty" and high-potential products first and compare your portfolio with the high-volume products of the market. Inspect your sales density in Q1 and Q2 and determine which customers are buying the entire product line and which are cherry-picking your portfolio. Look at how the contribution margins for the "eighty" products compare. Also look at how much customization you are providing, and ask yourself whether it is done on the behest of the "eighty" customers. The key here is to ensure that your "eighty" products are receiving differentiated attention from the business in terms of sourcing, marketing, sales, and logistics.

Then shift your attention to simplifying the low-volume products. The two most valuable strategies, based on my experience, are separating the "twenty" products and using a screening process to keep new part numbers from entering the system without the appropriate scrutiny. Commercial separation means that you raise the price of an item and sell it under different terms and conditions, such as different lead times and perhaps even payment terms. Physical separation includes running production on low-volume lines, outsourcing, redesigning certain products, and even dropping marginal products from the portfolio altogether.

Creative strategies surface when the task force performing the PLS is truly multidisciplinary and has engaged participants from different areas. When a few "eighty" customers require a certain level of customization, for example, manufacturing team members may be able to devise a way to tailor a standard high-volume product at the end of the line (postponed customization). The engineering members may be able to redesign one product to perform the function of two or more products, for example. At the end, sales and marketing members need to consider what else should be pruned or eliminated at the bottom of the CP matrix where the sales density is very low.

Over the years while working with different companies, I have seen significant results from the PLS tool that have reduced the number of SKUs they sell. Depending on the original size of the portfolio, the low-volume parts have experienced reductions between 5 and 25 percent after the initial project was completed. As the work progressed and teams became more experienced, I saw dramatic simplifications of portfolios, reducing the number of low-volume products manufactured in-house and SKUs by as much as 70 to 80 percent, with double-digit sales growth and profitability following.

Figure 9 shows the multiple strategies used to simplify the product line based on the 80/20 CP matrix. The underlined strategies are considered the most important in terms of their effectiveness for reducing complexity.

**Complexity reduction strategies based on the CP matrix:**

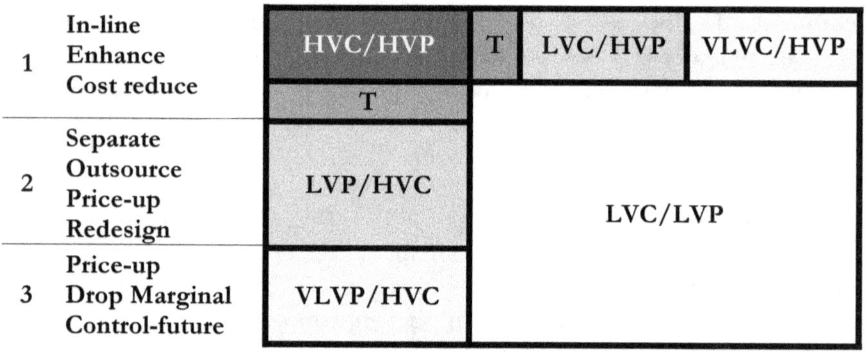

| | | | | | |
|---|---|---|---|---|---|
| 1 | In-line<br>Enhance<br>Cost reduce | HVC/HVP | T | LVC/HVP | VLVC/HVP |
| | | T | | | |
| 2 | Separate<br>Outsource<br>Price-up<br>Redesign | LVP/HVC | LVC/LVP | | |
| 3 | Price-up<br>Drop Marginal<br>Control-future | VLVP/HVC | | | |

Figure 9.

The control-future step (zone three) in figure 9 is central to avoid creating new part numbers that are not in line with the unique value propositions (UVPs) of the BUs. As with the separation phase, this process should not be restricted to zone three (the very low-volume products). Any new product entering the development process needs to go through a two-step screening process, such as that shown in figure 10.

**Filtering new product introductions:**

| FIRST FILTER | |
|---|---|
| **STRATEGIC FILTER** | -New market segment?<br>-Aligned with the strategy? |
| **YES or NO** | -Evidence of good margins? |

**+**

| SECOND FILTER | |
|---|---|
| **CONDITIONAL FILTER** | -New customer?<br>-Can it become "eighty" someday? |
| **YES, BUT** | -Financial targets?<br>-Manufacturing fit? |

Figure 10.

The first filter in figure 10 is a deal breaker that evaluates the product's strategic fit. It asks whether the new product or part number aligns with both the needs of the "eighty" customers and the BU's UVP. It also tries to understand the contribution margin potential early on. It asks why a new product should be added to the portfolio and what types of evidence prove that it will make money.

The second screening stage is conditional, establishing how the company will position the product to meet its profitability targets. It asks several questions: What is the minimum contribution margin acceptable? How are we going to price the new product? If the BU is creating a "twenty" product, is it done for an "eighty" customer? How are we going to create availability? Can we produce it using an existing manufacturing line? Should we create availability by outsourcing this product?

No product change request or new product charter should be approved without going through this screening process. Companies with effective screening processes have clear product complexity metrics that indicate how many new requests have been approved or rejected and provide a clear vision of the new product development pipeline. These metrics keep track of the numbers of products, part numbers, and SKUs that are eliminated from the system each month.

I need to acknowledge the fact that organizations are often resistant at the beginning of the PLS process. There are two main reasons for this resistance:

1.  Fear of losing the market position, sales, and customers.
2.  Fear of and resistance to change, with doubts and questions: Are we jeopardizing our business? Are there enough benefits? What happens if I do not succeed? Who will help us?

As with any major change, it is critical to articulate a vision of what can be accomplished with PLS. There needs to be clear and abundant internal communication. Managers also need to sell the idea of the final simplified product internally and externally. The program must be sold to the channel or to distributors, to key customers, and to end-users with the focus on what is in it for them. And slowly roll out the program—be aggressive but realistic on the timeline, and measure progress constantly in the number of parts added and deleted, the number of new products rejected and approved, and the size of the development pipeline. One of the best ways to sell PLS internally to the company is to show everyone the cost of having too many products.

## The Uneven Cost of Too Many Part Numbers: An Example

In many cases, it is useful to estimate the cost of complexity. People need to see and relate to the problem in order to get involved in the solution. There are many ways to estimate the cost of complexity, but one of the best ways, in my experience, is to calculate the impact of product proliferation on the overall cost of goods sold (COGS).

In this example, a tier one supplier of suspension components to car manufacturers sells a steering arm that needs to be redesigned or tweaked for virtually every new vehicle model or platform. The supplier hasn't figured out a way to offer an easy-to-understand product line architecture that allows a match between existing steering arm designs and new vehicle suspension designs. Since the steering arm is the last link between the suspension and the knuckle (that attaches to the wheel), a new design is almost always required before the development is completed. In other words, the steering arm is the last part addressed before development is complete.

At a certain point in time, the supplier has 110,000 different part numbers released and being produced in their system, with virtually every symptom of product line complexity present. An 80/20 analysis shows that 20 percent of the parts account for over 80 percent of the sales (no surprises here), while a significant number of the low-volume and special parts have very slow sales and are constantly showing up in obsolete inventories. New parts enter the system every day without any discussion through new releases and product change requests (PCRs). The "twenty" are interfering daily with the production of the "eighty" (high-volume parts).

The unfiltered variety requires more engineers to design, release, produce, and maintain the parts. From the manufacturing side, the high number of low-volume items requires the majority of production to be done in small batches, leading to an inflated number of line setups and changeovers. Tooling maintenance costs are sky-high. Feeding the line with raw materials is getting increasingly more complex, and more indirect people need to be present on the shop floor. This complexity also creates many problems for inventory control and aftermarket availability of these low-volume parts, reducing customer service levels.

The company's conventional cost accounting, using full absorption methodology, cannot fully capture the cost of complexity associated with the low- and high-volume parts. It can only distinguish the variable and the average COGS, using a standard allocation methodology, which lacks precision since it spreads the production cost evenly throughout the "eighty" and the "twenty" parts. The company's monthly profitability is at the mercy of the mix of products being produced and sold. If the company produces and sells more "eighty" parts, there is greater production cost absorption and profits are up. If the mix is unfavorable, leaning toward more "twenty" parts, the income statement or P&L will show the impact of lower absorption from additional changeovers, indirect manufacturing costs, and increased burden rates due to more indirect costs being applied to the direct labor or inventory. The contribution margins are reduced, and indirect shop floor costs go up over time.

After changing from the traditional manufacturing-cost accounting (absorption costing) to a direct costing method, the company arrives at the conclusion that there are significant cost differences between low- and high-volume parts. There are also significant differences between the production costs that are accounted for and the clean-sheet costs, which reflect the ideal cost arrived at through value analysis engineering. In this real life example, the differences between these costs, using the direct costing accounting, are significant. See figure 11.

**Clean-sheet cost does not capture the cost of complexity:**

## Average Product Cost

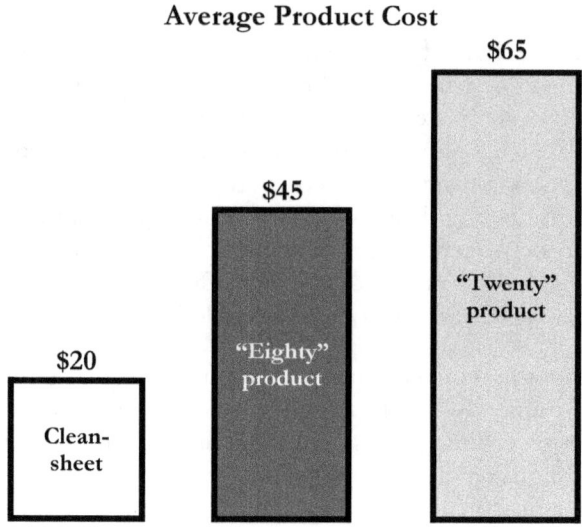

Figure 11.

The company used a clean-sheet-based cost model to determine the detailed "should cost" for each product. Using this clean-sheet cost as a base, we find that the average cost for a "twenty" part is 3.25 times higher than the base, while the average cost of an "eighty" product is 2.25 times more than the base. The "eighty" cost is being contaminated by the overall complexity of the large variety of products. This is one of the key reasons that separation between the "eighty" and the "twenty" products is so important.

In this example, the total COGS reported in the income statement in a given period amounts to $5 million. We then calculate the ideal or clean-sheet COGS multiplying the total number of parts produced by the clean-sheet-based cost of twenty dollars per part. We arrive at the clean-sheet COGS of $2.2 million dollars. From this, we can estimate the cost of complexity to be the difference between the COGS reported in the P&L and the clean-sheet COGS. The resulting estimated complexity cost is $2.8 million dollars. We can then estimate that each of the 110,000 part numbers costs, on average, an additional twenty-five dollars and forty-five cents due to the overall complexity, as shown next.

| Reported COGS in the Period: | $5,000,000 |
|---|---|
| Calculated Clean-Sheet COGS: | $2,200,000 |
| Complexity Cost in the Period = | $2,800,000 |
| Number of Parts in the System: | 110,000 |
| Average Complexity Cost per Part = | $25.45 |

If we then create a cumulative chart containing the individual cost of complexity for every part number, it will reveal the exponential nature of the cost of complexity (see figure 12).

**Cost of complexity goes up with part number count:**

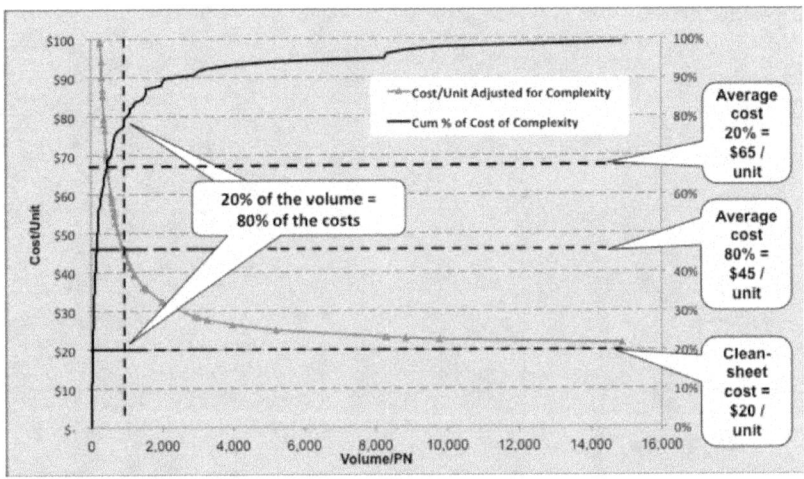

Figure 12.

The cost per unit, adjusted for complexity, tends to equal the clean-sheet cost, as the production volume per part number increases. An important and expected, although not very intuitive, conclusion here is that 20 percent of the volume is driving 80 percent of the cost. As the production volume per part number increases, the cost per unit tends to remain more stable and leave the turbulence zone where there is great disparity between the unit costs of high- and low-volume products. The very nature of this disparity points to a large improvement opportunity for this company. It shows that the company is not getting value for managing the complexity for the customer.

The question then becomes how to fix this and improve the bottom line using PLS. In this case, the business took several actions that improved the overall profitability and significantly reduced the number of discrete parts in the offering. They now offer approximately thirty thousand part numbers, a reduction of more than 72 percent.

The biggest drivers of simplification were pricing for complexity and a clear understanding of the customer's needs, in terms of how they use the product and how it relates to parts proliferation in the system. Customers were given the choice to use a standard part or a special part, with the caveat that special parts have special prices, which are adjusted for complexity. Some volume, mainly on low-volume items, was lost to other suppliers (12 percent in this case); however, the customers that remained loyal and paid for the complexity more than offset the lost volume. Eventually the market found a way to balance the offering versus the complexity costs.

# CHAPTER 5.2
# BUSINESS PROCESS SIMPLIFICATION (BPS)

Business processes are designed to create value for both external and internal customers of a company. As complexity increases, processes can become stifled and more oriented toward serving functional areas of the business as opposed to serving the end customers of the original process. They lose objectivity and acquire a life of their own. On the fringe, unfocused business processes can become means to their own ends. Bureaucracy, rework, delays, extra steps, more people, and endless attempts to automate rather than simplify are all signs of inefficiency.

Complexity drivers include a common distortion related to certain organizational structures, where functions and departments have a tendency to sequester key processes over time and make them more functionally driven than customer driven. There is a lack of balance between what is required by the company and the environment versus what is required by the end customer. The work and the results end up taking a backseat to standard operating procedures and other exogenous requirements. BPS provides the right forum and tools to regain balance and to the change the process orientation from being functionally driven to being result or process driven, helping regain customer focus and reducing complexity and costs.

Figure 13 depicts the evolution from functionally-driven processes to customer-driven processes. Customer-focused processes should be the backbone of all business activities.

## From functionally-driven to customer-driven processes:

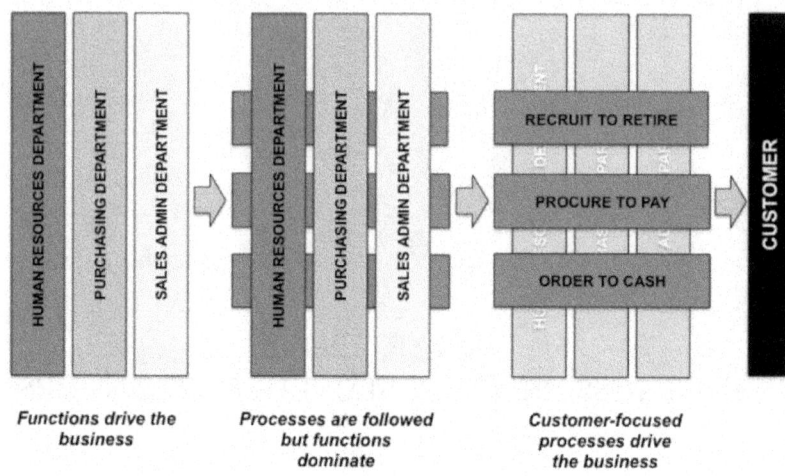

Figure 13.

Each department or function leads one or more key processes. By focusing on the value created by key processes (e.g. order to cash) instead of functions (e.g. sales department procedures), managers can streamline the BU and reduce overhead. To refocus, simplify, and improve efficiency, companies resort to different business process improvement tools such as process reengineering and six sigma.

80/20 uses commonly available tools, such as business processes mapping, with a high dose of 80/20 thinking and a focus on complexity reduction. It is particularly effective when the solution to improve the process calls for the application of information technology or process automation. In general terms, BPS is composed of three major phases:

1. Learning:
   • Observe, learn, understand, benchmark and draw the "is map", which reflects the current state of the process.
2. Simplifying:
   • Analyze, explore and draw the "should map", which represents the future state of the process.
3. Implementing:
   • Test and rollout the changes.

## Steps to simplify business processes:

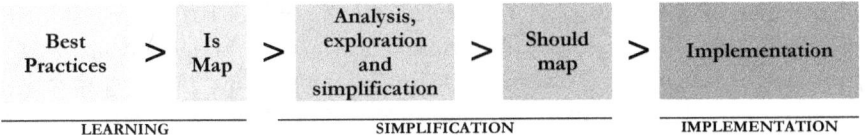

Figure 14.

BPS is a widely used methodology—it is simple to apply and yields results almost every time. The key for success is to identify complexity areas in the overall process flow and simplify them before you act or change the entire process, so emphasis must be given to phases one and two in figure 14. This greatly reduces the risk of failure during changes. BPS provides an organized project approach for simplification and assists in software selection if the answer points to automation. The expected outcomes for BPS should be the following:

- Fewer steps per process
- Less time per process
- Less complexity across the board
- Successful, on time, and on-budget projects

To prioritize and select which business processes to optimize first, managers should consider both their value to the business and the implementation complexity. A simple decision matrix to help think about priorities is shown in figure 15.

## Decision matrix to prioritize BPS projects:

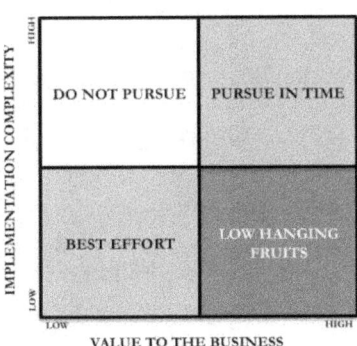

Figure 15.

Implementation complexity is dependent upon a series of factors, such as number of process users, functional scope, impact that changes might have on the business, organizational culture and budget available for making the changes. Picking the "low hanging fruits" means that you should work first on the "eighty" processes or those processes that are simpler and easier to solve, but at the same time, have a relatively high importance for the company. Applying "best effort" means that you should work on the "twenty" processes when you have time and resources to spare, since they have lower relative value for the organization.

## Learning with Process Mapping

Process mapping is a pictorial representation of the sequence of actions that comprises a process. In other words, it illustrates a process flow by showing how the work is actually done instead of how it should be done. It provides an opportunity to learn about work that is being performed. As Dr. Myron Tribus from MIT says, "You don't learn to process map, you process map to learn." Most processes today are left undocumented, so be prepared to spend time observing and asking questions. The general steps used to prepare the map of how a process is currently being executed are as follows:

1. Assemble the BPS team and a management steering committee.
2. Agree on which process you wish to map based on the decision matrix (figure 15).
3. Agree on the purpose of the process.
4. Agree on the map's beginning and ending points.
5. Agree on the level of detail to be displayed.
6. Start by preparing a narrative outline of steps.
7. Identify other people who should be involved in the process map creation (asked for input or to review drafts as they are prepared).
8. Map what is happening, not what you would like the process to be.

BPS teams can be set up differently depending on how critical and complex the project is. For major, complex projects that are hard to implement, I recommend that a management steering team be formed to guide and support the core user team. Core user teams are generally composed of process users who have full knowledge of the details, possess good communication and organizational skills, and most importantly, are open to change.

An opening workshop should be held to train all team members, to present a case study, and to plan for execution. Planning involves developing the project's work plan, setting goals, defining scope and deliverables, and establishing a timetable and communications approach. If possible, the team should take the time to visit a business that has successfully implemented a BPS project. For a complete view of the phases to draw the process map, see figure 16.

**Steps to develop the "is map":**

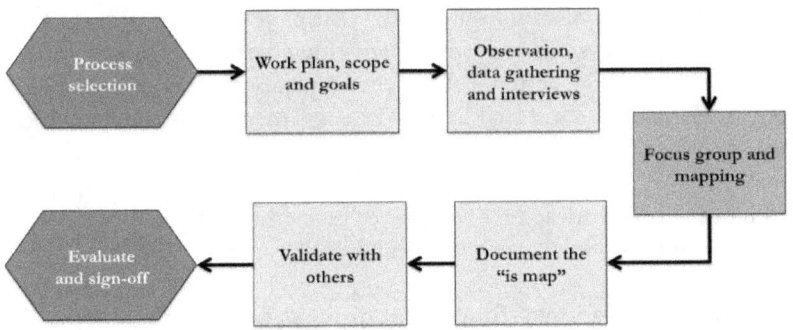

Figure 16.

After planning and observing how the process is actually done, the team develops documentation and creates a process map using the "brown paper flow" or the "is map." "Is maps" describe activities that transform inputs into outputs. The team should map the actual process the way it occurs and not the ideal process or the standard operating procedure. Here are some key questions to ask in the learning phase:

-What major activities are involved?
-What decision points and approvals are required?
-What sources of rework or waste are in this process?
-What factors inhibit process members from performing well?

Each and every step in the process should be recorded on its own sticky note and placed in sequence vertically (in the order in which they occur). Key process data should be gathered for each step, such as value-added and non-value-added times, sample documents, reports, screens, and digital photos.

Process inputs can also be classified into one of these four categories:

- N—Noise factors (uncontrollable)
- C—Controllable factors (can be changed to control the output)
- S—Standard operating procedures (set ways to perform a task)
- CF—Critical factors (keys to determining an outcome)

The sticky notes should then be placed under the area or person whose primary responsibility it is to complete it until they accurately represent the process flow. Appropriate flowchart symbols are associated with each step, and the activities between steps are shown using connectors. Shared responsibilities are highlighted in the process flow using circles and lines.

Figure 17 provides an example of a cross-functional process map, using the standard flowchart symbols and connectors.

**An example of a cross-functional process map:**

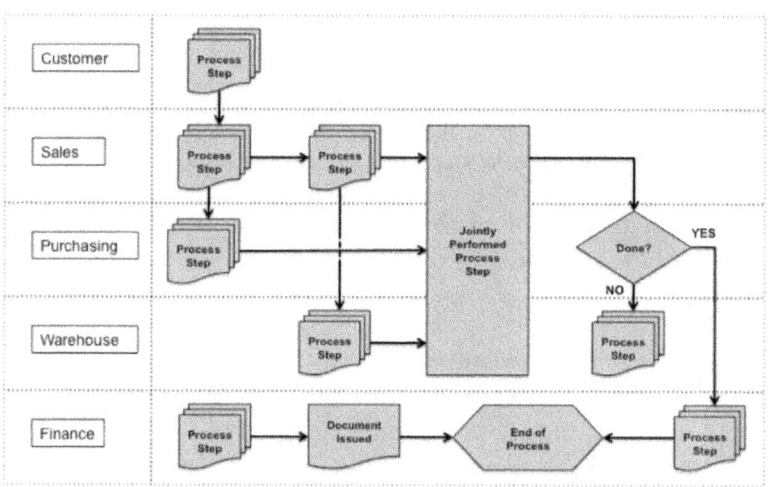

Figure 17.

Once the "is map" is completed and validated, the team moves on to analyze the process flow and its data in order to attack complexity and create a "should map". The core team organizes a workshop, with input and analysis from different sources, as shown in figure 18. Ideation and innovation workshop group work tools are always helpful during this phase. They can be found in the innovation section of this book.

**Elements required to develop the "should map":**

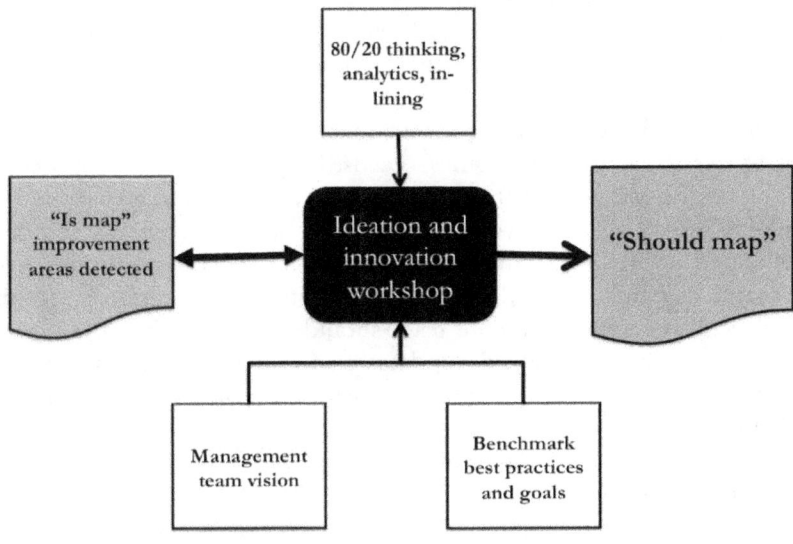

Figure 18.

The Deming Cycle or PDSA cycle is an often-used workshop tool to guide the work of this phase (see table 15).

| | |
|---|---|
| **PLAN** | What are you trying to improve? How will you make changes to bring about the improvements? How will you measure the improvements? |
| **DO** | Have a detailed implementation plan. Pilot and test the changes first. |
| **STUDY** | Observe and study the results from the changes. Ask yourself what happened and why. |
| **ACT** | Use what you have learned to take action. Apply lessons beyond the scope of the current project. Make adjustments to your improvement plan and try again. |

Table 15.

When analyzing the is map for complexity areas and streamlining opportunities, look for the following:

- High-volume transactions or steps within a process (e.g. activity and cycle times, activity flow that goes back and forth).
- Redundant activities and delays between steps.
- Unnecessary process steps, role ambiguity, bottlenecks or backlogs, and endless loops where rework is common.

Once you have finished your analysis, you can begin to brainstorm unique ways to handle the business needs, brainstorm how the procedure would look if it was set up from scratch, and segment and group the steps of the "is map". Gaps between best practices and benchmarks should be documented and highlighted in the "is map". The core team also needs vision and guidance from the management steering committee regarding the desirable outcome. The core team should meet with the steering team on a regular basis and provide updates and recommendations for policy changes. Another important point is to ensure the core team is applying the 80/20 principles to simplify the process:

- In-lining principles.
- Product line optimization principles to reduce the number of items, codes, vendors, prices, etc.
- Visual systems.
- 80/20 rules (focus on the "eighty" and treat the "eighty" different than the "twenty").

They should also be reviewing policies that create complexity, looking back into the business from the customer's point of view, and asking employees and customers what is complex. This will be valuable information for the creation of the "should map". At the end of the mapping exercise, and on top of the "should map", you need to compile the following information:

- Documented processes, highlighting the problem areas.
- Documented analyses of the root causes of the main problems.
- A list of recommended improvements.
- An outline of the main differences and gaps between new processes and best practices.
- Implementation plans.

### Getting Ready for Implementation

The team will know they are ready to implement their changes when everyone feels the workflow has been greatly simplified. Time and steps have been taken out of the process, and the majority of the listed issues have been resolved. The team members should have strong consensus that they are not just duplicating an old, complex process but that they are making it a lot simpler. It is also very important that they have conducted a trial or pilot to try out the new procedures.

One of the possible outcomes of simplification is the conclusion that you need to automate the process (by acquiring some new piece of software, for example). If that is the case, my experience points to a series of precautions to ensure the focus is really on improving overall value to the customer as opposed to adding more complexity and cost.

If the solution is automation, here are the do's and don'ts to keep in mind:

| DO'S | DON'TS |
|---|---|
| Develop weighted requirements for selecting the software. | Expand the scope of the process. |
| Follow best practices for software selection. | Modify the software (off-the-shelf is preferred). |
| Test-drive the software before you buy it. | Purchase software until after the BPS user team has done a scripted test. |
| Have the BPS user team and the IT department jointly select the software package. | Let the IT department select the package alone. |
| Develop and work off a detail task timeline. | Buy more power or capacity than you actually need. |
| Train those who will train others on the software. | Act alone; this is a team effort. |
| Conduct a minimum of three conference room pilots (CRPs). | |

BPS is especially effective for decisions involving information technology because it connects tool selection and implementation with process mapping and simplification. BPS increases the amount of time and focus allocated to testing versus traditional implementation strategies. By doing this, BPS raises the probability of a successful implementation. Traditional software selection processes allocates more time to selection and implementation. BPS, on the other hand, concentrates time and focus on testing in conjunction with the new and optimized business process.

There are a number of reasons major process changes and new business system implementations fail. Here are the top ten:

10.    Having unrealistic deadlines
9.    Dealing with company politics
8.    Automating bad processes
7.    Lacking prioritization
6.    Losing the management's commitment
5.    Lacking a formalized process for system implementation
4.    Not involving the right people up front
3.    Having badly defined or unrealistic expectations
2.    Lacking communication
1.    Underestimating user training

In conclusion, BPS is not a one-time event. BPS is a best practice and needs to be constantly applied within the BU. It only works with a clearly defined project, and it requires top management buy-in as well as committed and trained end user teams.

# CHAPTER 5.3
## PRODUCT AVAILABILITY SIMPLIFICATION (PAS)

I've covered portfolio optimization using the CP matrix and the PLS (product line simplification) tools. In this chapter, I will discuss how to create a sourcing strategy based on the CP matrix, define alternatives to produce what's in your optimized portfolio, and show you how to make these products available to your different customers. This portion of the methodology helps you decide what to produce and how to make it in-house as well as what could be outsourced to external suppliers. The CP matrix is the starting point to develop a custom sourcing roadmap that best fits your company.

**Sourcing strategy starts with CP matrix:**

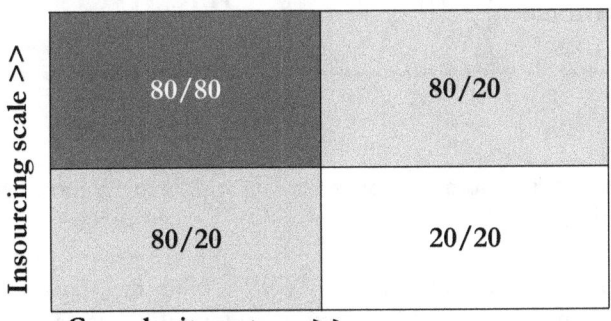

Figure 19.

The y-axis of figure 19 shows the product insourcing scale. The further north a product is on the y-axis, the higher the probability of attaining gains and economies of scale when making these products in-

91

house or insourcing. Toward the bottom of the y-axis, there is less and less scale, leading to considerations regarding availability, including outsourcing production to external suppliers or even eliminating the product altogether.

Moving right on x-axis, there is increasing complexity in dealing with the low-volume customers, primarily those buying low-volume items (the Q4 area) on a regular basis. The combination of product volume and customer variety can be seen as a proxy for complexity and helps the thinking around PLS pricing and sourcing.

Figure 20 shows that, when you take into account the transitional products and customers, you can draw three distinct areas or zones in the CP matrix. Note that the boundaries are not rigid since they depend on the peculiarities of each business.

**Different strategies for each zone of the CP matrix:**

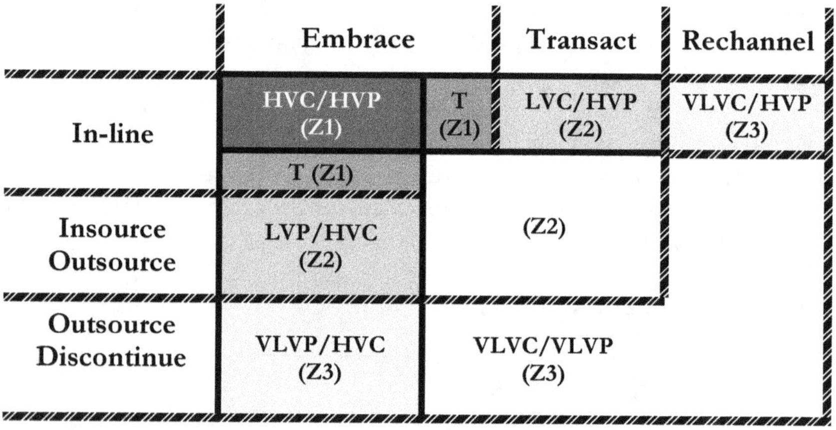

| | Embrace | | Transact | Rechannel |
|---|---|---|---|---|
| **In-line** | HVC/HVP (Z1) | T (Z1) | LVC/HVP (Z2) | VLVC/HVP (Z3) |
| **Insource Outsource** | T (Z1) LVP/HVC (Z2) | | (Z2) | |
| **Outsource Discontinue** | VLVP/HVC (Z3) | | VLVC/VLVP (Z3) | |

Figure 20.

The three major areas or zones in the matrix have the following characteristics:

1. Zone 1: Contains Q1 (HVC/HVP) plus the transitional products and customers (T). Production is done in-house and in-line, in the most efficient way. Customers are embraced and cared for in special ways, as they are considered the company's most valuable assets.

2. Zone 2: Contains portions of Q2 and Q3 plus a smaller portion of Q4. Production is typically insourced and done in conventional

production lines, separate from the "eighty". Some products are outsourced. Terms and conditions with customers are different from "eighty" customers when transacting. The complexity of doing business in this area should be reflected in the price (yes, but…).

3. Zone 3: Contains very low-volume areas of Q2 and Q3, and the remainder of Q4. This is where you outsource or discontinue the product from your offering. The goal is to reduce the size of this area. Many customers will be rechanneled to other customers and will no longer deal directly with the company. Pricing is the key mechanism to deal with this area.

The strategies by zone are summarized on Table 16 below.

| ZONE | STRATEGY | DEFINITION |
|------|----------|------------|
| Z1 | In-line | The production methodology used for high-volume products (the "eighty"); similar to one-piece-flow. |
| | Embrace | The approach used with strategic and high-volume customers to secure their loyalty. |
| Z2 | Insource | A conventional production methodology used for segregated low-volume products (the "twenty") that are manufactured in-house. |
| | Transact | The approach used to do business with low-volume customers, using differentiated commercial terms to compensate for complexity costs. |
| Z3 | Outsource | A production methodology that uses external suppliers to produce low-volume or noncore products that are sold to the customer base. |
| | Rechannel | The approach used to direct low-volume customers to buy from other high-volume customers instead of directly from the company. |

Table 16.

A typical CP matrix shows similar revenues or volume-density patterns within each zone, as exemplified on figure 16. But similar to the portfolio optimization process, we don't necessarily have to use a single sourcing strategy for each zone. When you consider zones two and three together, for example, you could very well uncover major outsourcing opportunities in either one. At the same time, there could be legitimate reasons revealed by the PLS tool to phase out products in both zones two and three.

I will now cover the strategies to create product availability for all three zones—in-lining, insourcing, and outsourcing. Keep in mind that these are typical approaches that are not exclusive to any particular zone. As I discuss production methods for zones one and two, I will briefly cover the MRD (market rate of demand) concept, given its significance to in-lining. I prefer not to explore in detail every manufacturing aspect or materials management methodology that is already widely known and documented, such as those in lean or TPS (Toyota Production System). I will only make reference to these tools and let you explore on your own, since I don't want to lose the unique thread of the 80/20 BPI.

## In-Lining Production

When it comes to zones one and two, the focus and best resources should be redirected to the "eighty" to keep them from being contaminated by the "twenty's" complexity. Here are main goals for these zones:

1. Separate the "eighty" from the "twenty" physically (location, resources, and management).
2. Optimize the production of the "eighty" to attain best cost, quality, and delivery in the leanest way possible.
3. Simplify production of the "eighty" through visual controls, pull systems, and self-directed teams.
4. Develop accurate ways to measure direct costs for the "eighty" and the "twenty".
5. Outsource some of the "twenty" using the criteria discussed below.

As I mentioned, there is no preconceived formula to decide what to in-line, what to keep in house for low-volume production, or what to outsource. Each case is different. In general, each area or zone in the CP matrix receives different treatment. For in-house production, physical separation between high- and low-volume products is an important step of the process. Many companies have opted for different facilities and even different BUs to keep the "eighty" apart from the "twenty." It helps simplify the "eighty" manufacturing by reducing the overall complexity in the dedicated production area, with less material handling, less movement, and fewer people. The focus on fewer, high-volume part numbers, has several advantages:

-Increases speed and single piece flow.
-Realigns the supply chains for the "eighty" and the "twenty" .

-Enables direct costing method, revealing the true cost of "eighty" products, due to no or significantly reduced allocations to the high-volume area.

-Gives you the exact total cost for the "twenty" by default, since the low-volume products are segregated in a separate area or outsourced.

-Optimizes direct labor, quality, and safety costs and delivery times for in-line products.

The separate production processes for "eighty" and "twenty" products are very different, even if they are under the same roof. The "eighty" products need to be produced in what is called an in-line. An in-line is defined as a dedicated group of machines and raw materials laid out in a straight line that are required for producing a single product or a very similar family of products without setup by a single person or team of people, producing a single unit at a time by continuously performing all of the operations required to meet the demands of the customer in a timely fashion. The in-lined factory has the following characteristics:

-Self-directed work teams.

-Visual triggers.

-PLS (product line simplification) and focused in-lines.

-No production controls or schedules.

-Replenishment triggered by the shop floor.

-Trust, communication, involvement.

-Focus on single unit flow and speed (not on line efficiency and utilization).

The transition from traditional batch manufacturing to in-line manufacturing is key for the "eighty." But I cannot emphasize enough the importance of completing the first phases of the 80/20 processes—mainly the analytics, optimization, and PLS—before embarking on this endeavor. Without having performed these steps, and in the absence of 80/20 thinking and the commitment to change, I would recommend staying with the traditional process and going back to the first phase of implementation.

I use this caution because there are a few common misconceptions about in-line manufacturing. When we compare its benefits against other traditional and outdated manufacturing methodologies, we often apply the wrong measurements to determine its effectiveness. The conventional manufacturing process separates each step of production into different areas or departments and performs the steps at different times. The flow time is usually measured in terms of days or weeks. Under the outdated method, the emphasis is on keeping the machines running at all costs and on maximizing efficiency of the operators. This is in part driven by the absorption-cost accounting method, which incentivizes production managers to build for inventory and keep unabsorbed costs at a minimum. At the end, the conventional way simply transfers the allocated costs from the production line to the inventory, where they sit until the units are sold.

There is nothing wrong with using the traditional method, but we have learned just how much "at all costs" means in order to emphasize full utilization of the equipment. All the hidden costs from the conventional manufacturing process should have no place in the manufacturing of the "eighty" products. The key for the "eighty" is to fully understand the total manufacturing cost and not just the direct labor portion. In rare instances, operator efficiency sometimes declines, but the overall costs plummet.

Under the in-line method, the emphasis is on keeping the product moving until it is finished. Pace and capacity are driven by customer demand. Contrary to the conventional model, all the production steps are performed in one department, sometimes by one operator, but usually by a team of operators. Flow time is usually measured in minutes. The key differences between the conventional and the in-line methods are listed in table 17.

**Differences between conventional and in-line production:**

| CONVENTIONAL | IN-LINE |
|---|---|
| Separate departments. | Integrated teams. |
| Lots of inventory, lots of miles on the parts, slow movement. | One piece at a time. |
| Inspectors, schedulers, expeditors, setup people, engineers, supervisors, clerks, computers. | Visual scheduling systems. |
| Forecast building. | Market rate of demand building. |
| Poor communication. | Natural and continuous communication. |

Table 17.

In a typical "eighty" factory, you will see several in-lines with only a few operators and a high degree of process automation. But you will notice the absence (or small number) of computers or information technology systems that are used in conventional factories for production planning or shop floor accounting. Modern IT technologies such as parts imaging systems are normally present for the sake of producing quality. But shop operators are managing the input materials, sometimes directly with suppliers.

The finished products are stored nearby by SKU so everyone can visually observe the size of the buffer, which is continuously adjusted for market demand. The stores are replenished continuously until they are full, like the shelves of a supermarket. The pace of production is displayed on a light board above the line. If demand halts or slows for whatever reason, operators can turn off the in-line for a period of time without having to worry about lack of cost absorption or inventory buildup. Operators become more like process-system engineers as opposed to menial workers who handle repetitive tasks for long periods of time.

A typical in-line setup and the summary of the main characteristics of an in-line are represented on figure 21.

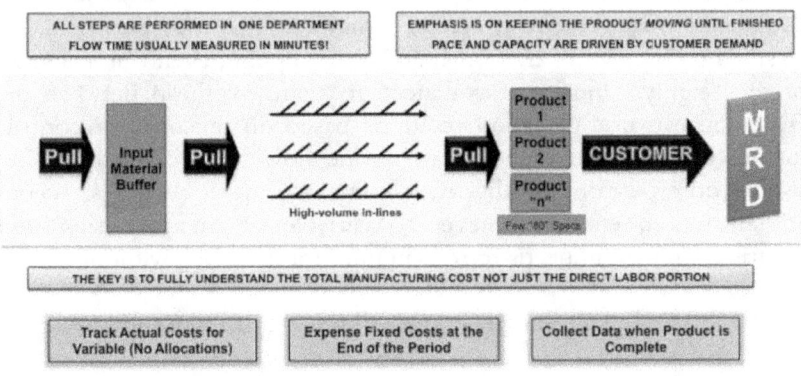

Figure 21.

Behind a wall or in a different building (or BU), you will find the "twenty" factory, which uses the conventional manufacturing methodology with two major differences: (1) it has a much-reduced number of SKUs versus a traditional portfolio and (2) it uses the direct costing method. There is a typical warehouse or store for low-volume finished goods. Since production is being driven by forecast, in batch mode, the company keeps a reasonable inventory of the shorter lead-time items (in most cases what I've been calling the products in zone two) in order to reduce the number of setups in the production line. Different lead times were applied during the planning process for customers and products. The low-volume products sold to "eighty" customers receive higher priority over low-volume products sold to "twenty" customers. At the same time, the lead times for the tail end of the "twenty" SKUs are proportionally longer.

The key advantage of having the high- and the low-volume products configured this way is that you know the exact costs going into each of the respective factories. It enables you to continuously focus on lowering costs, improving quality, and reducing delivery times for the "eighty," while you streamline the "twenty" and charge appropriately so that your company is properly rewarded for managing complexity for the market. Setting up both factories as BUs, with their own general managers and respective P&Ls, has other benefits since you are able to track the entire profitability and cash flow picture. This format also allows you to price products and differentiate your service levels in an all-inclusive way.

Having different BUs, even if they are under the same factory roof, will help you adapt to the ever-changing market conditions as products move from the "twenty" to the "eighty" and vice versa. It stimulates growth and segmentation thinking in the "eighty" BU, as well as allows better complexity management. It creates a mind-set that the "twenty" BU needs to stand on its own from a profitability standpoint, even if it is a subsidiary of the "eighty." Finally, if you need to share overhead between the two BUs, you can use allocation methods based on revenues or contribution margin dollars from each BU to decide how to split the cost. But this should only be done to the SG&A lines of the P&L (sales, accounting, administration, etc.) and never to variable or period costs, since the contribution margin needs to remain pure for each BU, without allocations.

## Determining Market Rate of Demand

In order to maintain a high level of production flow for "eighty" products through in-lining, we need a simpler and yet more effective materials planning methodology than the traditional materials requirements planning (MRP) system. This is where market rate of demand (MRD) comes in. To use a definition from ITW (Illinois Tool Works), one of the developers and largest users of 80/20, "MRD is a replenishment scheduling system based upon producing or replenishing products at the rate of demand. 'Demand' means actual consumption of products rather than forecasted consumption. If used correctly, MRD helps BUs to achieve high levels of customer service while helping to prevent inventory buildup and inventory shortages. The MRD approach to inventory replenishment and production scheduling is more effective than the traditional 'push' systems. Market demand dictates how many parts should be produced; therefore, materials are 'pulled' into production based on consumption."[xxvi]

Let's suppose for a minute that a company produces only one product and sells it directly to only one customer. In this extremely simple example, the customer rate of consumption would directly dictate the production cadence. The company would create some type of real-time sales refill mechanism that would drive the production pace all the way back to the suppliers. As most companies have multiple customers, buying multiple products through many sales channels and suppliers, they must account for many fluctuations in the rate of demand for each product as well as provide for variations throughout the entire supply chain.

Considering that we have already separated the "eighty" from the "twenty," we can apply this simpler replenishment system while bearing in mind that a limited number of SKUs generate 80 percent of the revenues. This system works like the refill method for supermarket shelves. In order to succeed, it must have the following elements:

1.  One-piece-flow manufacturing processes (in-lining).
2.  Production cadences compatible with the MRD.
3.  Visual replenishment signals available on the factory floor.
4.  Leveling of product mixes and quantities over time.

Each "eighty" SKU has its own storage area adjacent to the in-lines and the company maintains a specific quantity of product to meet the demand for that item, accounting for normal supply chain and market fluctuations. The in-line products go straight to their respective storage locations, replacing what is withdrawn until the storage bin is full. Production halts when the maximum level is reached.

## In-lines operate at the market rate of demand (MRD):

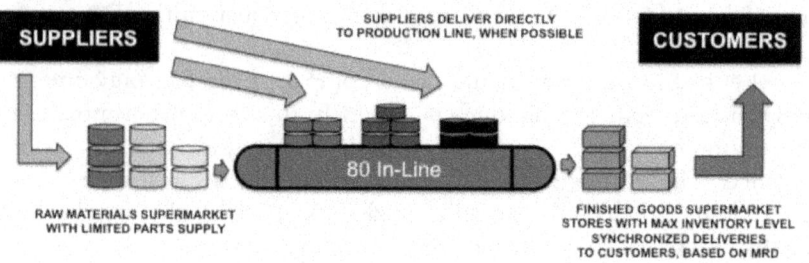

Figure 22.

The maximum inventory level required for each product is determined by synchronizing product consumption patterns with the production cadence of the in-line, accounting for delivery times from both internal and external suppliers. Planners collect commonly available data and adjust maximum storage levels as demand patterns change due to seasonality or other factors. The levels are constantly fine-tuned based on actual service levels to "eighty" customers. Typical data used to size the MRD stores includes the following:

-Historical usage or shipment patterns.
-Demand rates from "eighty" customers.
-Supplier data, such as lead times and replenishment cycles.
-Parts data, such as sourcing, unit costs, container quantities, and minimum order quantities.
-Current open customer order requirements.
-Current on hand, in-process, and in-transit inventories.

The initial calculation of storage capacity itself can take several elements into consideration to account for lead times and fluctuations:

-Average demand during replenishment lead time—this is the average amount of consumption from the supermarket that is expected to take place during the supplier's lead time to resupply.

-Deviation from average demand—this is the extra inventory required to cover variation from the average demand. Buffer stock amounts are based on historical average consumption and deviation from the average, factored for the rate of demand and required service levels.

-Average demand during the replenishment interval—the replenishment interval is the highest frequency with which the supplier can replenish the supermarket. This interval, when multiplied by the usage rate, determines the average quantity to be released or produced.

## Outsourcing the Low Volume

Make versus buy is a classic manufacturing dilemma. 80/20 offers a deliberate approach to outsourcing that ties back to central goals of reducing complexity and focusing on the vital few. The top reasons to look for outsourcing options are as follows:

1. Will let you focus on the "eighty," freeing and redirecting internal resources to work on the vital few.
2. Will reduce variable and fixed costs, eliminating the burden of capital or labor-intensive processes on the P&L and balance sheet.
3. Will reveal the true cost of the "twenty," revealing your variable cost as the invoiced price from the supplier.
4. Will reduce complexity, lowering the number of workers to supervise and eliminating hidden costs.
5. Will allow access of new capabilities and leverage of external expertise, adding value from capable external sources for the "twenty" to your overall marketing strategy.

The principal reason why managers resist outsourcing is due to the fact that they fail to realize the entire cost picture associated with low-volume products when comparing the internal cost of items to the prices offered by external suppliers. They often neglect to consider the hidden costs of complexity associated with these items, such as indirect and peripheral support costs that are not properly captured or are misallocated by traditional absorption-cost accounting methodologies. On many occasions, the variable cost of a product is compared with the supplier's quoted price alone, without inclusion of hidden complexity costs or even fixed costs.

Outsourcing the "twenty" takes a small leap of faith because you don't always know the full picture. You have to trust your instincts and have faith in the wisdom of the 80/20 principles. Shedding the "twenty" will have a multiplying effect on the positive side toward increased focus and profitability. As we saw above, outsourcing can be done in eithers zones two or three of the CP matrix.

Based on my practical experience, table 18 shows the key drivers behind typical make versus buy decisions, based on the CP matrix.

**Decision factors for insourcing and outsourcing:**

| INSOURCING | OUTSOURCING |
|---|---|
| All of high-volume products ("eighty") | A portion of low-volume products ("twenty") |
| Most of zone one | A portion of zones two and three |
| "Twenty" products sold at behest of "eighty" customers | "Twenty" products sold only to "twenty" customers (after PLS is done) |
| "Twenty" products that are considered "eighty" for the market or have the potential to become "eighty" for me | "Twenty" products that are high-volume products for the supplier (supplier specializes on the specific "twenty" products) |
| Items with sensitive intellectual property (IP) involved (in the product or process) | Items considered commodity products that are made by many suppliers (no IP involved) |
| Items with significant internal cost advantage | Suppliers with lower costs or better quality |
| Significant recent investment in process technology that cannot be recovered | Major new investments are required |
| No outside skills to offer a complete section of the portfolio | Supplier has significant skills (e.g., can provide a complete "twenty" portfolio ancillary to my core product line) |

Table 18.

A simplified decision tree for outsourcing is represented on figure 23.

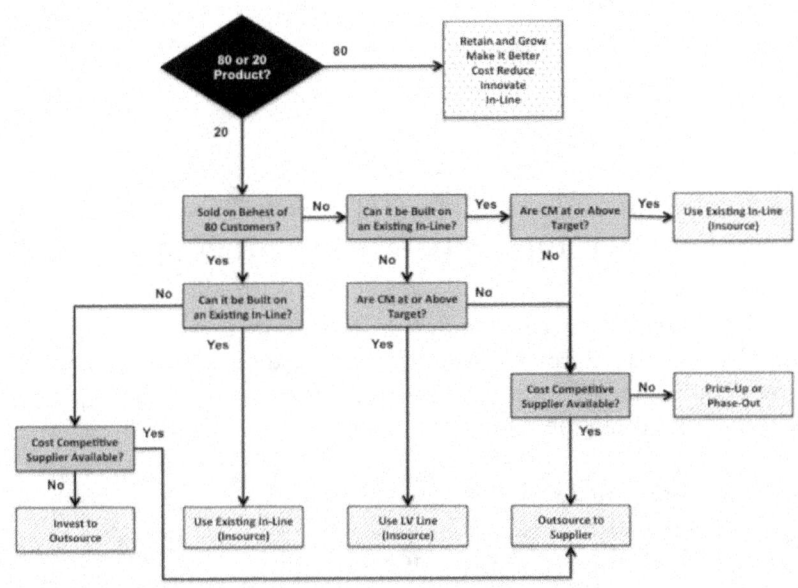

Figure 23.

While decisions to make or buy a product are deemed strategic, by applying the 80/20 methodologies properly, you will significantly mitigate the risk of a less than optimal decision on the "twenty." Even if you a make mistake, remember it will primarily affect the trivial many. Your key products and customers are protected and cared for in a better way. Once you have your outsourcing targets, a typical decision tree would look at whether the product is ancillary to the "eighty" mainstream or is an isolated low-volume item sold to low-volume customers. If any "twenty" item is important to the "eighty" mainstream (for example, a customer needs the complete lineup in order to sell the "eighty" product), sometimes you will have to go the extra mile to ensure it remains in your portfolio. You can either make it in-line (if you can follow the in-lining rules) or invest to put someone in business just to create availability of a "twenty" product that supports your "eighty" strategy.

# CHAPTER 5.4
## SIMPLIFYING THE METRICS

The metrics associated with the 80/20 BPI are aimed at reducing complexity and improving data accuracy and timeliness. They focus on three critical linked dimensions—margins, costs, and complexity. The benefits from using these metrics are as follows:

- Improved decision-making quality
- Improved focus on the big picture
- Close connection to 80/20 BPI
- Reduced complexity and costs associated with accounting
- Improved understanding through simple visual representations of data

Here are the most important indicators and areas to track in 80/20 BPI:

1. Contribution margin
2. Direct cost (simplified accounting)
3. Productivity
4. Complexity

Contribution margin tracking is such an important metric for 80/20 that it requires both a separate and a continuous focus. On a quarterly or even monthly basis, the BU updates the CP matrix and refreshes the quad analysis, showing how each quadrant has evolved in terms of sales and margins. The size and complexity of each quadrant is evaluated toward the goal of making quadrant one better and reducing the complexity of the other quadrants. A global productivity index is used to measure the overall performance of the BU. Complexity indicators are also included in the set of metrics to track simplification measures such as reducing the parts count and number of transactions. An overall or global complexity number (headache index) can be calculated as a benchmark between periods (refer to the section on complexity measurement). The income statement and free cash flow for the period, using the direct costing method, are included in the scorecard.

The metrics are designed to track the performance of market-segment-focused BUs related to 80/20 achievements. Other key performance indicators related to cost, quality, and delivery may be included in the BU scorecard as needed. Figure 24 is an example of a scorecard for a Business Unit.

## "xyz" Business Unit Scorecard

### INCOME STATEMENT ($ X 1,000)

| | |
|---|---|
| Revenue | $1,000 |
| Variable Cost | $600 |
| Contribution Margin | $400 |
| | 40% |
| | $100 |
| Period Cost | |
| Gross Margin | $300 |
| SG&A Expense | $100 |
| Total Overhead | $200 |
| Operating Income / EBIT | $200 |
| | 20% |

### QUAD ANALYSIS

| | Q1 | Q2 | Q3 | Q4 | Total |
|---|---|---|---|---|---|
| # Parts | 6 | 6 | 14 | 14 | 20 |
| % | 30% | 30% | 70% | 70% | |
| Revenue $ | $623 | $79 | $111 | $117 | $931 |
| % | 67% | 8% | 12% | 13% | |
| Units | 34.8 | 5.2 | 7.3 | 8.5 | 55.8 |
| % | 57% | 9% | 12% | 14% | |
| CM $ Total | $166 | $25 | $31 | $27 | $248 |
| % | 67% | 10% | 12% | 11% | |
| CM % | 27% | 31% | 28% | 23% | 27% |

### PRODUCTIVITY INDEX

PI = CM$/LABOR$ = $800,00/$100,00 = 8.0

### CASH FLOW ($ X 1,000)

| | |
|---|---|
| Working Capital | $150 |
| % of Sales | 15% |
| Free Cash Flow | $30 |

### COMPLEXITY METRICS

| | |
|---|---|
| Sales per SKU ($) | 120 |
| Sales per customer ($) | 300 |
| Sales per location ($) | 45,000 |
| Sales per employee ($) | 10,000 |
| Contribution Margin per SKU ($) | 40 |
| C.M. per customer ($) | 70 |
| Global Complexity Factor = | 630,000 |

Figure 24.

You will need to decide which set of metrics is best for your business. There are many options, but you don't want to create more complexity by adding new reports and measuring too many things. The old adage that you only improve what you can measure is still valid, so pick your vital few metrics wisely based on what the business needs to improve the most. To facilitate choosing the vital few metrics that are right for your business, I have divided them into different categories. In general, contribution margin and direct costing are essential to adopt. As you move on to productivity and complexity, you have a few different options, depending on the challenge you have. These sections offer different angles that you can choose from to address specific issues.

## Contribution Margin

Contribution margin measures the amount that individual products or services contribute to net profit. It is a very important metric since it reveals a key comparison that otherwise would lie hidden in the income statement. In fact, it represents the most important decision tool to direct or redirect resources within the company. Knowing the contribution margin enables managers to make better decisions regarding launching a new product, entering a new market, pricing an existing product, acquiring a business, or making investment decisions in general. Many businesses choose to only show the cost of goods sold (COGS) line in the P&L and jump directly to the gross profit margin. By doing this, they are missing out on the most important ratio between the market and the company.

### Calculating contribution margins:

| | PRODUCT "X" | PRODUCT "Y" | PRODUCT "Z" |
|---|---|---|---|
| Sales Price | $120 | $280 | $350 |
| Variable Cost | $72 | $196 | $273 |
| Contribution Margin $ | $48 | $84 | $77 |
| % | 40% | 30% | 22% |

Table 19.

Table 19 shows how to determine a product's contribution margin by subtracting the variable cost from the sales price. Product $X$ generates a higher contribution margin percentage, even though products $Y$ and $Z$ have the potential to generate greater revenue and profits in dollar terms. Sales strategies can be designed to increase the mix of product $X$ and improve the margin of products $Y$ and $Z$. If this data is laid on top of the 80/20 CP matrix, it becomes even more relevant, since we will want to apply our limited resources to improve the contribution margin of the "eighty" products or sell more of the "eighty" if the margins are already healthy. Note that this information is not visible in a standard income statement showing only COGS and gross profit margin.

This simple, powerful ratio lies dormant inside the income statements of many companies and is not fully utilized at the individual product or customer level for the simple reason that managers do not trust the data. In most cases, the data is polluted with inaccuracies from allocations and estimated costs that have little to do with the specific reality of a single product or service. Yet it is the most important way to measure the financial performance of an individual product or service.

Another way to look at contribution margin is to think of it as the correlation coefficient between the external environment (the market) and the internal structure of the company (differentiation ability, vertical integration, etc.). In other words, there are both external and internal forces driving the contribution margin. When BUs superimpose the contribution margin dollar CP matrix over the revenue CP matrix, they will have a visual representation of the contribution from each quadrant of the market segment. If the same exercise were done for the number of transactions or the SKU count, the BU would have a reasonable picture of the complexity cost compared with revenues and contribution margins.

External forces are things like market structure, competition, and pricing power (or the power to command higher prices in a given segment). Some markets are saturated, so the ability to price up a product or service for improved margins is fairly limited. Other markets have plenty of opportunity for flexing prices. In the case of selecting new markets to enter, managers can make better decisions if they understand the level of contribution margin that can be expected or is being seen in that market today.

If feasible, gathering market intelligence on contribution margins on top of more traditional competitive data before entering a market segment is the best approach. This is highly recommended for critical product launches, where the business should tear down competitor's products and estimate the amount of added value using value-engineering tools. If nothing else, material margin is a good proxy for contribution margins and will provide the business with a solid knowledge on the current level of contribution margins in the market. We should then ask this question: Is there evidence in this market that one can reach a defined level of contribution margin? Selecting the right market or segment to join is just as important as having the right product cost to compete.

Differentiation versus the competition is another aspect impacting contribution margin. Unique products and services have greater pricing leverage compared to commodity products. This is the key reason why segment-focused innovation is such an integral part of the 80/20 BPI. When customers recognize true value of a product or service, they will reward the company with higher contribution margins.

Internal forces determine the ability of a company to impact the variable cost of a product or service. In many instances, companies can charge different amounts at different times to attain higher contribution margins. These companies have an economic moat for being a low cost producer. Many factors are at play here, such as the use of in-lines for the production of high-volume parts, the strength and the level of vertical integration of the supply chain, as well as the ability to continuously drive cost out of the product or process through material and supply chain optimization processes.

The ability of a company to profit adequately from a product or service starts with sound contribution margins. There is almost nothing managers can do to improve the profitability of the business if there are poor contribution margins to begin with. Cutting overhead costs alone will not achieve the goal. The only way to correct this situation is to work very hard to achieve healthy contribution margins. On the other hand, having healthy margins to begin with gives managers great flexibility and maneuverability. 80/20 is a methodology to improve and manage contribution margins by focusing on a small number of variables.

If contribution margin measurement and tracking are so important, how do we accurately determine the contribution margin of each product? The answer lies in two fundamental principles of the methodology. First, the "eighty" products must be physically separated from the "twenty" products. And second, a direct costing method need to be used. Separation is covered under product availability simplification in chapter 5.3, and the direct costing methodology will be presented in the next section. But it suffices to say that the "eighty" are so important that they require special treatment to reveal the variable cost with greater accuracy.

Managers sometimes believe that selling a product with a positive contribution margin, regardless of its level, can be accretive to or that it will not hurt overall profitability. They want to keep the production lines moving at all costs. However, this is not always the case in companies that use cost-absorption accounting methods, since they almost always neglect to account for the cost of complexity associated with sales and manufacturing. Only when the "eighty" cost data is gathered in a direct way and is not contaminated by the complexity costs of "twenty" products can a manager really affirm that a positive contribution margin is accretive.

## Direct Costing

Back in the 1980s, when the United States was coming out of an energy crisis and an inflationary period, businesses recognized that there were going to be fewer and fewer opportunities to increase prices. At the same time, costs would continue to increase so that only low cost producers that were focused on profitable market segments would survive. Taking cost out was an imperative. At the shop floor level, a lean revolution was starting to take place, inspired by the successes of Japanese car manufacturers like Toyota. Unfortunately cost accounting systems were not evolving at the same speed. Even when manufacturing was converting from batch production to single piece flow, cost accounting was still unchanged.

Collecting data at every operation and adding cost to inventory at each stage of the production process was the modus operandi. There were a myriad of people assigning standards and creating formulas to spread costs throughout the manufacturing operations. Labor efficiency and machine utilization reports were sent out daily, and all manufacturing costs were included in the product cost. This method is called full absorption costing (or absorption costing). Unless a company was producing at a high level of efficiency and using most of their available capacity, they would be penalizing the product margins for lack of absorption. The problem is that full absorption costing incentivizes the wrong behavior in management. They tend to keep the lines running at all times, even if the market demand is not there, in order to attain high levels of absorption. Obviously, this behavior creates inflated inventories and drains cash from the business.

The full absorption costing method encourages labor and machines to keep working rather than inventory to keep moving. It was developed with mostly tax compliance and other fiscal rules in mind; it is suitable for external reporting and not for operational excellence. It was and is highly complex and inaccurate. It is also dissociated from real-time operations and is highly dependent on estimations. It encourages continued production for greater cost absorption as opposed to inventory flow and pull through. At some point, companies started to experiment with other methods that were more suitable to lean methodologies.

Activity-based costing (ABC) was a worthy attempt to apply lean principles to accounting methods. ABC borrowed the value stream mapping concept from lean manufacturing but still depended on estimations and was prone to inaccuracies. According to the Chartered Institute of Management Accountants (CIMA), ABC is "an approach to the costing and monitoring of activities which involves tracing resource consumption and costing final outputs. Resources are assigned to activities and activities to cost objects based on consumption estimates. The latter utilize cost drivers to attach activity costs to outputs."[xxvii] ABC is also expensive to implement (a bonanza to consulting houses and software developers), and its data is prone to being misinterpreted.

In order to become a low cost producer, operations need a simple and accurate cost accounting methodology that is capable of supporting efficient manufacturing processes with increased parts flows, reduced lead times, and minimal work-in-process (WIP) inventories. Such a method is called direct costing. It is not the same as activity-based costing. Direct costing is a better, more straightforward way to calculate the variable cost component of the contribution margin. It is better because direct costing is designed to focus on product flow and to measure what is actually happening on the shop floor without theoretical estimations. It captures exactly what is going into the transformation process and collects data only when the product is complete.

The old cost absorption method was based on job cost, with many work orders on every job, which increased the number of transactions and made it hard to see the big picture. It required a lot of central planning and production control, as well as many computer systems. It normally used direct labor hours to assign costs and fixed overhead to jobs at each operation.

On the other hand, direct costing does a few things differently to simplify the process:

- It expenses fixed costs in the period they were actually incurred.
- It uses no allocations of fixed costs to products, departments, segments, etc.
- It is visible as a stand-alone expense line item in the monthly P&L.
- It puts strong emphasis on contribution margins.

By accumulating and reporting fixed costs in the period and not spreading them arbitrarily across the products or hiding them in the inventory until the next period, direct costing keeps contribution margins clean. With this simple change, managers can focus on operational efficiency and rely on the accuracy of contribution margins to determine which products are contributing to profitability. Other benefits of direct costing include the following:

- Data collection is simplified, reducing the number of transactions and associated costs.
- More accurate nonfinancial shop-floor measurements are established, such as yield, scrap, throughput time, output, and customer service.
- Shop floors can use visual measurements and sees their contribution margins.
- Business process cost drivers are identified—purchasing, receiving, shipping, order entry, etc.
- Managers are allowed to focus on the process and not on dollarized absorption variances.

Table 20 shows a numerical example of a typical income statement for a business using direct costing. Note the lines referencing contribution margin and period cost, which replace the COGS line, used in conventional accounting. They give management a more detailed and real-time picture of the monthly results.

| INCOME STATEMENT ($ X 1,000) | |
|---|---|
| **Revenue** | **$1,000** |
| Variable Cost | $600 |
| **Contribution Margin** | **$400** |
| | 40% |
| Period Cost | $100 |
| **Gross Margin** | **$300** |
| SG&A Expense | $100 |
| **Total Overhead** | **$200** |
| **Operating Income / EBIT** | **$200** |
| | 20% |

Table 20.

The variable cost includes raw material, direct labor, and other costs that vary with production volume. Period costs include manufacturing management, building, production control, quality control, shipping, warehousing, insurance, depreciation, etc.

Comparing the old (absorption) and the simplified (direct) systems side-by-side reveals the information in table 21:

| OLD METHOD (ABSORPTION) | SIMPLIFIED (DIRECT) COSTING METHOD |
|---|---|
| Significant number of transactions at all levels (many are hidden) | Costs tracked to the cell (bucket) Cell controls inventory (when to build and when to purchase |
| Data accuracy issues | Variable costs expensed monthly in the cell (ties into total product produced) |
| Excessive data and complexity<br>- Manufacturing says accounting needs it to track costs<br>- Accounting says manufacturing needs it to track jobs and inventory | Reduced amounts of data and controls<br>-Fixed costs equal period costs<br>-Most transactions are eliminated<br>-Total is measured |

Table 21.

Under absorption costing, fixed manufacturing costs incurred during the period and not sold with the product during the same period will be placed in the finished goods inventory and will not show up in the P&L right away. They are deferred and carried on the balance sheet as part of the inventory account. This means that fixed costs are piled up in inventory and do not become variable product costs or costs of goods sold right away. Such a deferral of cost is known as fixed manufacturing overhead deferred in inventory. Companies have to hope that the inventory sells at just the right price so they can recover their costs in full. Figure 25 shows how this works.

**Conventional absorption cost accounting flow:**

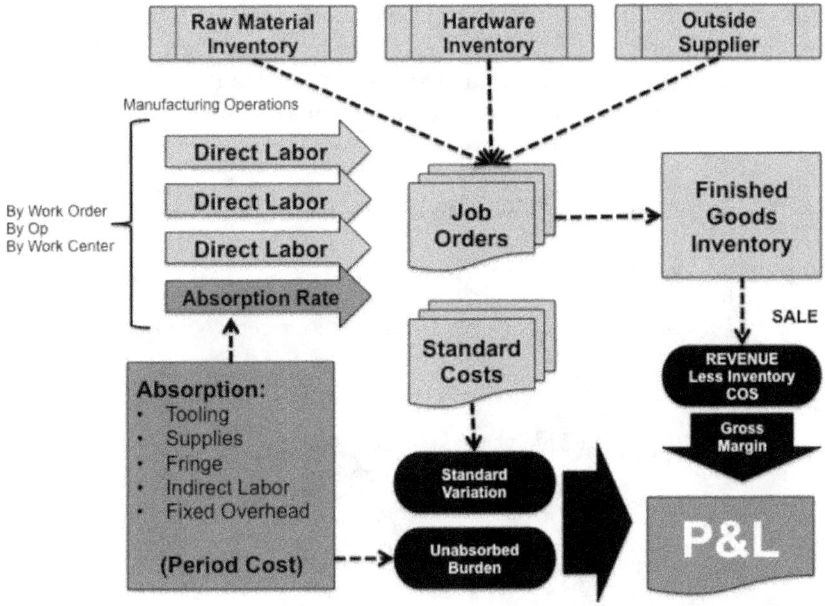

Figure 25.

Another potential issue with the full absorption costing system is the fact that it postpones the impact on margins when there is a market downturn or a reduction in sales. Companies have to wait until units are sold to see the full impact on the P&L and start taking countermeasures. Unless they use other metrics to know that costs have gone up in the inventory, the time lag between build date and sale date, when they realize they have a cost issue, will increase as sales slow down.

With direct costing, all fixed costs incurred during the period show up in the income statement right away. Since all fixed costs are loaded in the period, the bottom line tends to be smaller than that for absorption-cost accounting in the same period. It is better to have a realistic picture sooner than later. Direct costing shows what is really going on with the variable cost. There are no unreal margins or surprises down the road when inventories need to be adjusted.

On top of having too many transactions and increased complexity, the absorption-costing method does not differentiate fixed and variable costs, which creates confusion and errors during planning and control. Too much guessing and theoretical classification goes into the P&L when absorption costing is being used. Direct costing is like a real-time snapshot of what is going on in the period, without guesswork. It generates pure data that can be used more reliably for COGS calculations. Since there are no individual work orders, costs are accumulated in buckets for the period in question, and finished products are only accounted for after they are built (see figure 26).

**Cost information-flow with direct costing method:**

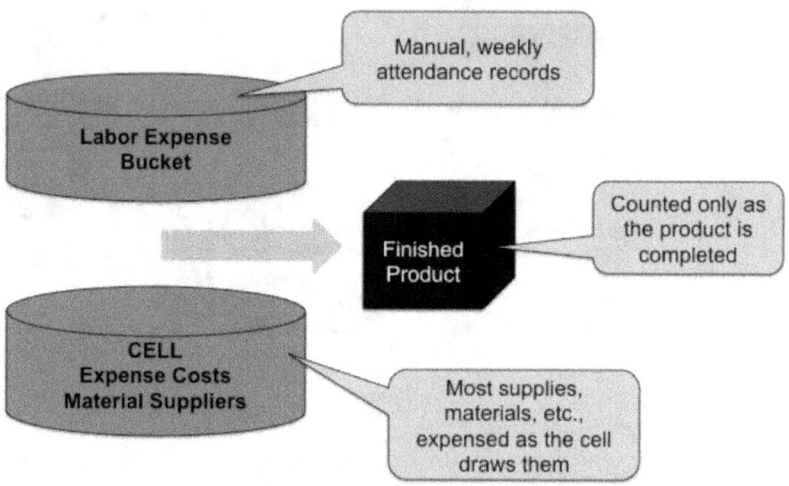

Figure 26.

Once finished products are complete, they are moved into the finished goods inventory at a standard cost. When they are sold, there should be no surprise on the margin, since period costs have already been taken to the income statement. There is no delay or data pollution. The pure contribution margin provides a more accurate picture of the variable cost, allowing for better decisions in terms of pricing and productivity metrics. Should the market slow down, actions can be taken right away to deal with the situation. There is no postponement of the information. Figure 27 shows the direct costing system.

**Direct costing method:**

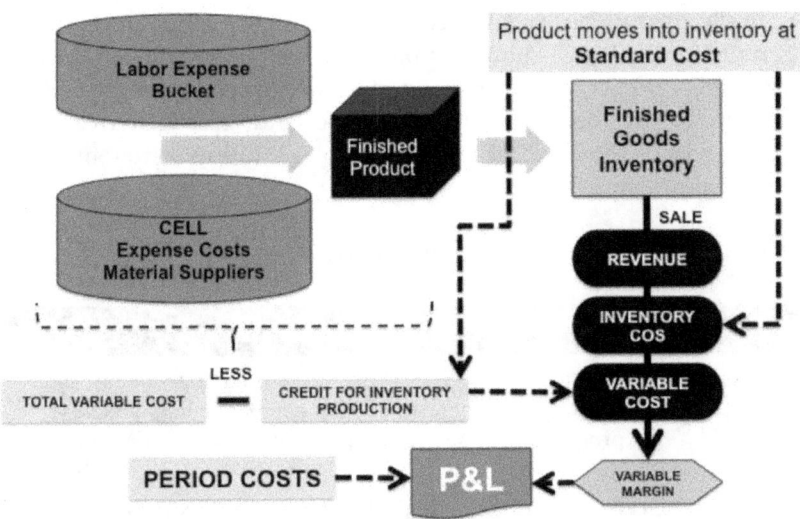

Figure 27.

In the direct costing method, all labor is charged to a generic work order or single bucket, which is closed monthly. No raw material, hardware, or semi-finished goods are placed in inventory since blanket purchase orders are used for each cell. All costs are lumped together in one general ledger account. The accounting department keeps monthly summary billing information from vendors. Work orders are only used when throughput is over thirty days. There is also the need for accounting to manage and account for working-process (WIP), so out-of-period costs don't distort cell performance.

Typical management reports for each operating cell include revenue and cost data (labor costs, cell expenses, contribution margins, incoming orders, throughput days, and inventory data (materials on hand (MOH), active, slow, obsolete). These reports are typically visible at the shop floor.

Conversion to direct costing requires adjusting the recorded value of individual inventory items to their variable costs and creating a period costs in inventory account to capitalize the period costs associated with the inventory on hand. Period costs must be capitalized to ensure that total inventory value reflects total actual cost. Period costs in inventory must be adjusted at least quarterly to ensure that total inventory valuation reflects total actual cost.

Direct costs vary 100 percent with production. They must be specifically identifiable and measurable, and they cannot be the result of allocations. All other manufacturing costs that must be inventoried are considered period costs. Costs that are not manufacturing costs and are not inventoriable are deemed selling, general and administrative expenses (SG&A) costs. Table 22 provides examples of how different costs are classified at the income statement.

**General classification of cost items:**

| COST | EXAMPLES |
|---|---|
| **DIRECT COSTS** | Rebates, freight (in and out), inventory adjustments, direct labor, fringe labor, direct material, packaging, outside processing, royalty expenses, scrap, production utilities |
| **PERIOD COSTS** | Depreciation, premium freight, tooling, insurance, inventory reserves, maintenance, quality control, inspection, manufacturing support, disposal, outside services, period cost adjustments, rent, restructuring, warehousing, supplies, taxes, general utilities, warranties, workers' compensation |
| **SG&A** | Insurance, bad debt provision, commissions, customer service, employee activities, engineering, finance, HR, legal, marketing, office supplies |

Table 22.

If direct costing is so much more accurate and reliable than absorption costing, why is absorption still used in large scale? The answer lies in the observation that direct costing works better in a lean and efficient manufacturing environment. Wherever there is lack of empowerment on the shop floor, low- and high-volume production running together, slow flow, a waste or lack of visual and simple-to-follow metrics or where there are too many unique operations, you are likely to see an absorption costing methodology being used.

When the shop floor is not in control of its work, then businesses need many external, indirect people walking around estimating ways to spread fixed costs throughout operations and departments. And since this was and is the way that many manufacturing companies operate, it produced an entire industry of accounting, consulting, and complex big-ticket customized IT systems.

## Productivity

Productivity is generally defined as a measure of output per unit of input. Broadly, BU productivity is defined and measured in terms of a ratio that is calculated as the total value captured from the market segment over the total value of resources being applied (see figure 28). Productivity can be thought of as the inverse of complexity. The more complex a BU is, the less productive it is (and vice versa).

$$\text{PRODUCTIVITY} = \frac{1}{\text{COMPLEXITY}} = \frac{\text{TOTAL CONTRIBUTION MARGIN \$}}{\text{TOTAL LABOR COST \$}}$$

Figure 28.

The productivity index in figure 28 (also called GM2 or gross margin two) takes into account the total contribution margin dollars for the period divided by the total labor cost for the same period (direct, indirect, and SG&A-relate expenses labor). 80/20 BPI increases productivity by reducing complexity and optimizing contribution margins. Highly productive companies utilize six levers to improve their productivity indexes:

1. Manufacturing productivity creates product availability using 80/20 methodology (in-lining, 80/20 separation, "twenty" outsourcing, etc.).
2. Overhead reduction properly reallocates resources to serve Q1 and the BU segment.
3. Supplier collaboration lets companies work with suppliers to reduce costs and improve product performances.
4. Supply chain optimization improves logistics, service levels, and product availabilities, aligning the production of high-volume parts with key suppliers.
5. Design-to-value method aligns product design with market requirements and pain points.
6. Complexity reduction lowers the numbers of parts and transactions, directly and positively impacting the bottom line.

The power of productivity resides in the fact that it has more leverage to impact profits than sales increases do. For every dollar gained there is an equal amount of profits flowing directly to the bottom line. It would take three times that amount in revenue increase to obtain the same effect on the P&L, assuming a contribution margin of 33 percent.

## Complexity

Complexity-cost accounting and tracking have been neglected by managers and accounting systems for a long time. Many businesses do not have metrics around complexity since, as discussed in the direct costing section, conventional accounting systems hide the cost of complexity deep in their operating statements and inventory. Direct costing begins to address part of the issue by displaying period costs at the end of each period so managers can deal with them in a timelier manner. For the purpose of understanding the origins of complexity costs, I will classify its drivers and metrics under five areas.

1.  Organizational structure complexity develops when too many layers of management and control in a complex matrix-type organization are created by structural mitosis and well-intentioned initiatives to centralize common functions in the company. Mergers, acquisitions, and the global nature of business make the situation worse. The problem can be solved by decentralized market-focused BUs using segmentation to grow organically. This formula is used by the best-performing companies in the world, such as Berkshire Hathaway. These global, complex companies operate with simplicity. Recommended metrics include a global complexity factor (GCF) that accounts for multiple drivers of complexity in the business. It should be applied at the BU and overall company levels.

2.  Market structure complexity comes from looking for growth in convoluted and disorganized markets. It is very common in emerging economies such as China, India, and Brazil. It can also be caused by failed segmentation or by misunderstanding the market's needs. The complexity is based on the fast pace of change in the segment and also on unforeseen buying patterns from customers. The solution is to use 80/20 analytics to target the "eighty" customers and become more aggressive about weeding out the "twenty" customers and products. In emerging markets, it helps to have a local partner to sharpen the focus on the vital few customers. Recommended metrics include a productivity index for the segmented BU (see figure 28), a record of the number of transactions per customer, and a measure on the dispersion of sales volumes across the customer base. Businesses should refresh the CP matrix and quad analysis more often in these situations.

3.  Product variety complexity comes from a poorly architected product offering. A portfolio with too many SKUs and part numbers coupled with unmanaged customization and a lack of a process to screen out new products that are not aligned with the segment strategy will produce product variety complexity. The solution is the application of 80/20 analytics, CP matrix optimization, and product line simplification (PLS). Recommended metrics include a productivity index applied to the number of SKUs or products in the portfolio. This will show how much pure contribution margin dollars the market is paying for each product in your portfolio.

4.  Transactional complexity comes from the quantity and quality of administrative and operational processes driven by internal and external complexity. The lack of a disciplined focus on process efficiency, such as BPS (business process simplification) or six sigma, will also produce this type of complexity. The solution is to segment the business into decentralized segment-focused BUs and apply 80/20 BPS. Recommended metrics include tracking overhead costs and the number of internal transactions associated with key processes.

5.  Supply-chain complexity comes from the prevalence of outdated manufacturing, logistics, and supply systems that do not take into account the complete alignment of all the vital few assets and elements in the business. The solution is to apply 80/20 analytics, CP matrix optimization, and PAS (product availability simplification). Recommended metrics include calculating process-cycle efficiency (PCE), which is the ratio of total value-added time over total lead-time in the supply chain. It can also be defined as an index, in terms of total contribution margin dollars over total period cost dollars. PCE is highly connected to complexity, since adding new products without improving cycle times will decrease PCE and increase complexity costs.

Table 23 shows examples of complexity metrics for each category.

| CATEGORY | METRIC EXAMPLES |
|---|---|
| **Organizational Structure** | 1. Global complexity factor (GCF) = (number of customers + number of suppliers + number of employees) X (number of SKUs X number of locations) |
| **Market Structure** | 2. BU productivity index (GM2) = Total contribution margin $ / total labor cost $<br>3. Sales by customer<br>4. Contribution margin by customer<br>5. Transactions by customer |
| **Product Variety** | 1. SKU productivity index = total contribution margin $ / total number of SKUs<br>2. Sales per SKU<br>3. Total number of SKUs<br>4. Number of SKUs added and dropped during the last period |
| **Transactional Complexity** | 1. Overhead productivity index = total contribution margin $ / total SG&A $<br>2. Cost to process a customer order (end-to-end)<br>3. Cost to process a purchase order (end-to-end)<br>4. Cost to set up and maintain a product SKU<br>5. Cost to serve by customer<br>6. Purchase transactions per vendor |
| **Supply Chain Complexity** | 1. Process cycle efficiency (PCE) = total value-add time / total lead time<br>2. Supply-chain productivity index = total contribution margin $ / total period cost $ |

Table 23.

Product variety and number of sales transactions are good proxy indicators for complexity cost. A worthy exercise is to superimpose the transaction and the product variety CP matrices on top of the contribution margin CP matrix. A very common conclusion is that complexity cost is distributed unevenly over contribution margins and revenue dollars. The quadrant sizes and shapes are not proportional. This means that a company's efforts and resources are being applied in an average rather than a selective way. It also means the business is on the perverse side of the 80/20 natural law and that there are large improvement opportunities.

In this case, the business needs to focus on reducing the number of transactions and the product variety associated with quadrants two, three, and four. Complexity costs are high in areas that don't matter as much. The problem is that all this cost is wasted effort in the wrong direction.

# CHAPTER 6
## FOCUSING ON SEGMENTATION

Top-line growth is essential for the long-term viability of any business. Growing more slowly than market rates or relatable economic sectors can be a significant problem. Companies also need to increase profits in proportion to revenues (or ideally faster) as they grow; however, the greatest challenge to growing a business profitably resides in the fact that additional revenues can bring along additional complexity and extra costs. If profitable growth is not executed in a lean and efficient manner, cash flow is impacted and future earnings are compromised. So the question is how to profitably grow the business in the leanest way possible. The 80/20 method says that you should start by looking inside your current markets to find new growth avenues before you branch out into unknown areas. Exhaust adjacent or incremental growth near the core business and then look for growth beyond the core, such as new markets and mergers and acquisitions (M&A) initiatives. Consider tapping into the fractal behavior of your current markets first to uncover new ways to deliver customer value at the lowest cost.

The segmentation portion of the methodology is about helping companies sharpen focuses on profitability and growth through a proven approach to leverage the wealth that they have already acquired—their existing customer bases and product portfolios. The process starts by dividing customers and products into new segments, categories, micro markets, or niches to gain new insights into pain points and needs. With new and in-depth understandings of the markets, BUs can develop unique value propositions (UVPs) for selected segments through innovation. Businesses apply intense management focus to targeted segments and attain growth with the least amount of waste. By using segment-focused BUs built from the ground up, the expansion costs are kept closely coupled with the business's ability to deliver and charge for the value in the UVP, minimizing the need for corporate overhead. Everything needed to grow and profit in the new segment should be included in the BU's P&L.

The 80/20 method combines segmentation and growth while relying on the natural laws of fractal behavior and evolution. Fractal behavior is the principle behind segmentation, which ensures there is always more to be gained by sharpening the focus on niches and subsegments within your existing customer base. Coupled with evolution, it drives the value creation continuum embedded in the 80/20 implementation cycle—analyze and optimize, simplify, segment, and grow. Once a company reaches a size where it is too complex and losing focus, then it's time to optimize and segment again. If a business applies the value creation continuum enough times under a systematic innovation framework, the business will evolve and develop a wide economic moat. Evolution, as I will discuss in chapter 7, will drive transformational growth, taking companies beyond the existing core and incremental businesses and creating an economic moat to fend off competitors and new entrants. The natural evolution principles for segment-focused BUs are what define the segmentation continuum.

I like to compare the continuum to the reproduction and growth cycles of life-forms in nature. Each individual has unique abilities that impact their chances for growth and survival, and they all require different amounts of support or stimuli to develop their full capabilities. But in order for a species to survive and grow, individuals will have to reproduce and form or join communities. Since there is no way to know exactly which individuals or communities will succeed, nature will add diversity to the mix and be prepared to change course if necessary. The community provides the basic support and the environment for continuous growth of the species in a way that, if one individual is not capable of growing on its own, the association with other individuals will provide the means for it to move forward. In our case, a failure in segmentation can lead to reincorporation of that individual BU back into its parent entity. The interesting analogy is that the parent BU that generates one or more subsegments is also changed for the better since it gains extra customer focus. So in a sense, the parent is a renewed and improved unit once it generates another segment. Market-segment-focused BUs are the individuals in the 80/20 business community.

## Segmentation Case Study: HDV Brakes

HDV Brakes is a fictional manufacturer of aftermarket air brakes and air brake repair components for heavy-duty vehicles. Its customer base is comprised of a number of retail parts distributors and a number of large fleets, including both trucking companies and city bus companies (mainly public transit authorities). Over the years, the sales and customer-support people came to learn about the differences in how end users apply their products between the various types of vehicles. The product's duty cycles (or the ways the customers use the products) were very different. City buses have a much higher number of stops or braking events compared to over-the-road trucks; therefore, buses require many more service stops to repair the brakes.

All bus fleet customers had similar pain points in relation to brake repair frequency, but end users were not able to clearly articulate the issue since they did not have a good comparison basis. Transit authorities usually have control over public transportation in a given city. The sales and support people accumulated enough data to know there was a marked difference in the consumption patterns between customer types. They also frequently visited service shops and talked to maintenance people and discovered there was an unspoken pain point related to the frequency of brake repairs in fleets with bus and specialty vehicles. HDV decided to conduct a few innovation workshops to find a solution for what they perceived to be a problem for some of their customers. The result was the development of a more robust repair kit for city buses with the potential to reduce repair frequency by more than 30 percent. The company was able to validate the new product with several bus customers and came to the conclusion that the UVP was compelling enough that customers would pay more for the new kit versus the normal truck-based kit.

After marketing the new product line for six months, HDV decided to conduct a segmentation study to see whether it would make sense to create a separate division to market to transit authorities. The number of differences, in the way of doing business, between these two segments was growing. HDV completed a segmentation analysis and launched a new commercial segment, splitting the sales team into truck and bus customer groups.

The change was well received by bus fleets. The sharper, more specialized sales focus drove new selling behaviors, such as providing training to install the parts and helping fleets calculate the total cost of ownership and the return on investment (ROI) for the new, more expensive kit. HDV knew that it had a new UVP, as sales and profits grew on both commercial segments. The "eighty" truck customers were now receiving more attention and focus and were also offered the option to buy the upgraded repair kits. The truck sales force was interested to notice that heavy-haul and specialized over-the-road fleets were also interested in the bus kits. These customers were very much into reducing service intervals and managing their total costs of ownership since they had a much more severe duty cycle than over-the-road truckers.

After one year of running these two commercial segments in parallel, HDV compared the results with the original goals and decided that it was time to move on to phase two—physical separation into two independent BUs. However, the unforeseen interest in the new kit from other truck fleets drove HDV to rethink the scope of each segment and to create a new BU that was dedicated not only to bus fleets but also to severe-duty trucking fleets that needed specialized brake repair kits. These fleets were primarily made of vocational or specialty trucks. They created two BUs— HDV Truck Brakes and HDV Severe-Duty Brakes. This expanded scope for the new BU beyond city bus customers was not evident during the segmentation analysis. It only came up during the implementation of the commercial segmentation phase.

The severe-duty BU evolved to become fully specialized in reducing vehicle downtime and improving total cost of ownership of brake products for bus and vocational truck fleets. Having its own production line, albeit at a lower volume than the truck BU, allowed them to focus on reducing the cost of the "eighty" kits ("twenty" for the truck BU) while getting a premium on the sales price by creating application-specific features. The return on sales (measured in terms of earnings before interest and tax - EBIT) grew faster than revenues and quickly compensated for the added resources necessary to create a full-fledged BU.

From my personal experience after having done this a number of times, you will not really know the full potential of segmentation until you test your UVP in the marketplace. You may end up with a different scope than what you had in mind when you started. The other benefit is that segmentation frequently leads to new growth opportunities that would otherwise lie hidden under the original segment. In the case of the HDV Truck Brakes BU, it pointed to potential segmentation based on the type of distribution channel, for example, parts retailers versus service outlets. Once you embrace the fractal principle via segmentation, you will gain additional insights into new levels of the market.

## Segment-Focused Business Units

A segment-focused BU is a separately managed division or unit of another major division or enterprise with a mission and objectives that are both distinct from the parent unit and integral to the overall performance of the enterprise. The BU is created to focus on a specific market segment that requires management focus and specialization not contained elsewhere in the parent organization.

BUs are unique as they represent the operating arms and legs of 80/20. Everything else in the enterprise or the parent company should exist in support of the BUs, so the BUs can place strong focus on their missions. To grow and thrive, they need four elements: (1) a well-defined market segment to serve ("eighty" customers and "eighty" products), (2) a UVP, (3) singular business model with an innovation process that goes beyond product, and (4) an intensely focused management team.

Applying the 80/20 process to the BU will promote growth and increase profitability over time. In almost every case, there is additional revenue to be found as you keep drilling into the "eighty" of the "eighty." However, all four elements or BU pillars need to be strong every time you segment. This operating model depends on management focus and decentralization, as we can see reflected in this quote from a 1979 letter from Warren Buffett to investors, which talks about his faith and confidence in the independence and empowerment of BUs. The thinking can be summarized in this statement: "If you love the management, set them free".

*"To the Shareholders of Berkshire Hathaway Inc.:*

*Your company is run on the principle of centralization of financial decisions at the top (the very top, it might be added), and rather extreme delegation of operating authority to a number of key managers at the individual company or BU level. We could just field a basketball team with our corporate headquarters group (which utilizes only about 1,500 square feet of space).*

*This approach produces an occasional major mistake that might have been eliminated or minimized through closer operating controls. But it also eliminates large layers of costs and dramatically speeds decision-making. Because everyone has a great deal to do, a very great deal gets done. Most important of all, it enables us to attract and retain some extraordinarily talented individuals—people who simply can't be hired in the normal course of events—who find working for Berkshire to be almost identical to running their own show.*

*We have placed much trust in them—and their achievements have far exceeded that trust."* [xxviii]

This powerful piece references to two other extremely important features and benefits of operating with market-segment-focused BUs. First is the ability to operate with paper-thin staffs at headquarters or at company division levels, since the operational authority and responsibility lies with the BU in general. Second, and maybe most important of all, is the ability to attract and retain the best talent available (the "eighty" talent) and to let them run their own shows. These are the types of jobs that are most appealing to the best managers out there. Behind the most successful companies of all sizes, you will find a similar, if not exactly the same, framework—empowered and independent BUs, extremely focused BU general managers and staff members, and ultra lean headquarter staffs.

The reason why so many companies get lost in complex organizational matrices based on functional areas is that they do not recognize the importance of simplicity and focus. They basically ignore the vital few natural laws in business and create artificial and unsustainable management structures that are self-perpetuating. More economic value has been destroyed under the labels of strategy or synergy than you can imagine. The multibillion-dollar enterprise-wide IT systems industry has pushed very hard against decentralization and empowerment. In contrast, 80/20 companies delegate the automation decisions to the BUs after the business units have simplified and optimized their processes. They almost always buy off-the-shelf software that costs a fraction compared to multimillion-dollar enterprise resource planning (ERP) systems, which have become in many cases a crutch and an excuse for a lack of decision-making at the operational levels.

Every for-profit enterprise exists to create value for a number of stakeholders, but before it can do that, it has to create value for customers and markets. This is why the best companies place so much emphasis on pushing most, if not all, assets and resources down to the BU level and closer to customers and markets—the ones paying for the value. For all practical purposes, this push down is a natural separation practice and the only realistic way to guarantee that companies are not creating complexity for the sake of complexity. This push down mind-set is also the best way to measure and track performance while reducing the risk of failure for the whole enterprise. These 80/20 companies have small, lean offices at their headquarter and division levels. They don't buy production lines or big-ticket computer systems or hire a lot of people. Their BUs deploy assets and hire people to do the work. The enterprise may buy companies that fit their overall strategy, but any new acquisitions will eventually fit under the same lean architecture.

Organizations using the 80/20 process plan for growth and development based on this decentralized model. They know that if they strengthen their BUs, they will be better prepared to deliver value to stakeholders. A well-functioning BU will almost always guarantee sustainable growth if it possesses talented leadership, a well-defined market segment focus, a strong UVP, and people and processes capable of innovating in the broader sense. I have witnessed great practices in strategic planning and succession development planning for BUs using this model. At this point, I will use the HDV Brakes Company to exemplify the four basic elements or pillars of the new segment-focused BU, serving the severe-duty market.

The types of decisions and questions asked during strategic planning have to do with the elements that determine success or failure of the BUs, outlined in table 24 below.

| PILLAR | CONTENTS |
|---|---|
| Structure | Strength of UVP |
| | Market segment focus and definition |
| Performance | Top-line and return on sales (ROS) growth |
| | Innovation results (revenues, patents, etc.) |
| | Segmentation potential and timing |
| Talent | Leadership development |
| | Development needs |
| | Succession planning for key positions |

Table 24.

**Example: four pillars of the a market-focused business unit (HDV Severe-Duty BU):**

| "Eighty" segment | UVP | Singularities | Leadership |
|---|---|---|---|
| North American Transit<br><br>Authorities and Specialty Truck Fleets<br><br>Market size = $.... million | The most durable brake repair kit in the market.<br><br>Designed for severe-duty and stop-and-go-fleets. | In-lines manufacturing, differentiated service support, customer engineering. | GM = John Smith<br>Ready now = …<br>Ready 2/3 years = …<br><br>Revenues = $... million<br>ROS = xx%<br>Five year CAGR = yy% |

Table 25.

The market-segment focus is sharp and well defined. The UVP is tested by the "eighty" customers in this segment and approved. The BU has its "eighty" production in-lines and a sourcing strategy for the "twenty" parts. The sales and marketing approach is unique and targeted at "eighty" customers. Innovation workshops are a way of life for the BU. The leadership is clear and the metrics are simple and well understood by everyone. I will now go into segmentation, and explain how to achieve this type of sharp focus on market segments.

## Segmenting the Business

There are five distinct phases when segmenting a business under 80/20: (1) deciding why and when to segment, (2) selecting the segmentation method, (3) planning for execution, (4) testing and validating the strategy, and (5) full implementation of the new BU.

129

**Segmentation phases:**

| 1 | Decision | - Reasons to segment the business<br>- Goals and objectives |
|---|---|---|
| 2 | Selection | - Segmentation bases and methods<br>- A priori and cluster analysis |
| 3 | Planning | - 5 P's (marketing mix plan)<br>- New segment analysis |
| 4 | Validation | - Commercial segmentation<br>- Validation |
| 5 | Separation | - Independent market-segment-focused BU<br>- Monitoring |

Table 26.

## Phase One: Understanding the Reasons for Segmenting the Business.

There are many valid reasons and benefits for segmenting a company's market into smaller segments and for sharpening the marketing focus, such as improved customer service, increased innovation, increased customer intimacy, and better communications. However, 80/20 goes well beyond the traditional marketing concept of segmentation, which aims to identify target segments and develop new marketing mixes and positions. This is why 80/20 uses a more structured process to identify and increase managers' confidence in the level of success of a new segmentation plan.

Once managers are confident about the growth potential offered by a sector of the current market, they should give extreme attention to the newly identified segment and provide the new BU with the dedicated tools and resources necessary to fully develop the business. The 80/20 process asks for a much bigger commitment to the segment than what is traditionally prescribed by marketing theory. In reality, 80/20 companies are primarily looking for increased growth, better margins, and reduced fixed costs when they segment a business, on top all the other benefits listed above.

The most frequent reasons used by 80/20 businesses to adopt full-fledged segmentation plans are as follows:

1.  Companies want to energize or reenergize sales growth—the ambition to expand the business into foreign markets, for example, is a proactive way to think about segmentation. Sometimes markets change, and a new segment may be created within a market where the company already has a meaningful presence. One example is the emergence of the DYI (do-it-yourself) segment in the home improvement industry. Many existing and new entrants, such as Home Depot and Lowes, developed entirely new business focuses and segments around DYI, including innovative products and new ways to do business. A business may also choose to segment when it is not growing enough or is falling behind the competition or the industry. In this case, segmentation unleashes the fractal power of the market and breaks the practice of treating all customers (and even competitors) as if they all behave in a similar way. Segmentation forces the evolution of the business model in this case.

2.  Companies want to profit on UVPs—companies with a high degree of customer intimacy, that are constantly looking for market pain points, will periodically come up with relevant innovations that can impact the whole or a sector of the customer base. In order to capture the full value of a UVP, companies opt to segment and use extreme focus to market the new solution. In the HDV Brakes example, the innovation of a severe-duty brake kit that lasts longer in city buses is compelling enough to prompt HDV to focus on the new segment that cares for the UVP. There is both a growth and a contribution margin opportunity in this example. The other common situation is when a company is not happy with the margins delivered by an existing product or UVP. In this case, businesses will look for a niche or a sector of the market that values the UVP higher than the average of the market. The typical examples are related to businesses that carry high up-front or elevated transaction costs for their products or services. They improve margins by being selective and only offering an existing UVP to segments of the market that are willing to pay more. Auto parts manufacturers selling to passenger car manufacturers are typical in this case. Some suppliers chose to do business only with those original equipment manufacturers (OEMs) that can value and price their UVPs adequately to the car buyers.

3.  Companies want to reduce complexity and cost—complexity increases in proportion to the number of transactions and the number of SKUs in the business, driving costs into the organization. Transactions are generally a result of revenue growth in ways that are not lean or connected with segmentation. As the problem grows, it might be

necessary to break the BU in two or more segments in order to intensify the attention to simplification and cost reduction. This is one of the reasons why 80/20 proposes separation between high- and low-volume products in the first place. We have all heard of companies that fail because they have grown too big and too complex to manage. In fact, there is a big debate going on right now regarding banks that are considered too big to fail. If they go under, they may cause a systemic failure to the broader financial system (similar to Lehman Brothers in 2008). A BU that grows too complex may fall into averaging customer needs and begin to create dissatisfaction instead of satisfying customer needs.

## Phase Two: Segmentation Bases and Methods

Markets present both fractal and diverse behaviors, and they are constantly changing. In order to deaverage the market and develop a UVP, businesses need to decode the natural diversity and break up the market in smaller segments that have more or less homogeneous characteristics. According to Philip Kotler, "Market segmentation is the subdividing of the market into homogeneous subsections of customers, where any subsection may conceivably be selected as a market target to be reached with a distinct marketing mix."[xxix] Market segmentation is the first step toward BU segmentation. The other steps are commercial segmentation and validation and physical or full segmentation into market-segment-focused BUs.

In conventional marketing strategies, the segmentation phase is followed by a target marketing phase (selection and validation) and by a market-positioning phase (how the products are portrayed differently in customers' minds versus competitors'). These phases are similar to the 80/20 approach to segmentation, but they differ on the implementation methodology for steps two and three. The 80/20 method provides much more practical and hands-on ways to test the efficacy of the segmentation hypothesis in the real market and then find more objective methods to create demand and deliver products and services to customers.

Segmentation requires market research and knowledge as well as 80/20 analytics. But before you decide which segments to target, you need to be clear about known rules and characteristics that segments must exhibit to be considered worth pursuing. Paul Green and Donald Tull[xxx] developed these four basic criteria for segmentation:

1. Exist in nature—the segments must exist in the environment (and not be a figment of the researcher's imagination).

2.   Identifiable—the segments must be identifiable (repeatedly and consistently).
3.   Stable—the segments must be reasonably stable over time.
4.   Accessible—the segments must be efficiently reachable (through specifically targeted distribution and communication initiatives).

I would like to include a fifth item on this list: the segment's size in terms of revenues and profits also needs to be substantial so the company can adequately structure a BU to serve it. In general, segments need to have measurable characteristics that are similar to a subset of customers within a market and yet are differentiable from the overall market.

With these features and conditions in mind, the next step is the segmentation analysis itself, which is divided in two types of analyses:

1.   A priori analysis is based on market research and knowledge. The BU classifies the customer base in accordance with generally accepted groupings.

2.   Post hoc analysis (also known as empirical phase analysis) is based on analytics and market research. A team creates several scenarios based on the segmentation bases established during qualitative study, with the help of 80/20 CP matrices.

There are unlimited numbers of groupings or bases to segment markets; therefore, the business should not limit its thinking to conventional bases. After companies engage in segmentation a few times, they tend to develop more refined industry-specific methods on their own. A manufacturer that is trying to segment the markets internationally, for example, is likely to use additional bases such as economic, political, and cultural factors in addition to geographic location. A more complete example of segmentation methods and bases is laid out in table 27.

| SEGMENTATION BASES | | EXAMPLES |
|---|---|---|
| Demographics | Industry | Light vehicles OEM, commercial vehicles OEM, aftermarket |
| | Company size | Large cap, mid cap, small cap |
| | Location | North America, Europe, Asia, south region, eastern region |
| Purchasing approaches | Region | Regional, national, or global buyers |
| | Time horizon | Long-term agreements, spot purchasing |
| Situational factors | Urgency | Planning practices, forecasting |
| | Application | Oil and gas, mining, over-the-road, power generation |
| | Order size | Blanket PO, small orders |
| Operating characteristics | Technology | Type of technology applied |
| | Capabilities | Level of proficiency in using the product |
| | Usage intensity | Severe duty, light duty |
| Personal Characteristics | Loyalty | Relationship level and degree of partnership |
| | Risk taking | Early or late adopter |
| | Buyer or seller | Relationship to the company, government, private sector |

Table 27.

The segmentation groupings also vary depending on whether you are trying to segment an industrial versus a consumer business. However, the key to this phase is to spend some time discussing all the potential bases that would apply to the specific business and then to use the group experience to determine the most likely a priori methods to be validated. Besides the five bases mentioned on table 27 (demographics, purchasing approaches, situational factors, operating characteristics, and personal characteristics), there are many other bases for business markets, such as product attributes, values, brand preferences and loyalties, price sensitivities, etc. A priori is a qualitative phase and a primer to the analytical phase; therefore, teams need to resist temptation and not jump to conclusions too quickly. A useful template with some examples related to the HDV Brakes case is shown in table 28.

## Example: segmentation template.

| METHOD | | SEGMENT | SEGMENTATION CRITERIA (3=YES, 2=UNCLEAR, 1=NO) | | | | |
|---|---|---|---|---|---|---|---|
| | | | Real | Identifiable | Substantial | Stable | Accessible |
| Demographics | Application | On-highway Trucks | | | | | |
| | | Specialty Trucks | | | | | |
| | | City Buses | | | | | |
| | | OEM | | | | | |
| | | Aftermarket | | | | | |
| Operating Characteristics | Usage | Light Duty -cycle | | | | | |
| | | Severe Duty-cycle | | | | | |
| Personal Characteristics | | Private | | | | | |
| | | Government | | | | | |

Table 28.

After selecting a set of initial candidates, 80/20 analytics are applied in order to complete a baseline segmentation study. The baseline will have the following characteristics:

-Includes both current and prospective customers and products:
- Large customers ("eighty" to market) not buying or classified as "twenty" customers.
- "Eighty" products to the competition, not sold by the company or in the "twenty" today. Uses a larger sample of data from 80/20 analytics to account for alternative bases. Longer time spans account for seasonality and market dynamics.

-Uses a large amount of time during data analysis to explore alternative methods and bases. Does not discard other hypotheses that have not been listed since the data may talk louder.

-Involves senior leadership early on to discuss alternative methods and bases.

-Collects factual market information as needed during the work:
- Profitable segments that are not being served by the company today.
- Competitive information on high-volume products sold by competitors (or sold by the company at low volumes).

The 80/20 analysis used at this phase is also called cluster analysis, since it looks at groups of CP matrices for each segmentation method. In the example above (table 28), the team would have four different clusters to evaluate—application, channel, usage, and buyer type.

## Example: Cluster analysis using HDV Brakes:

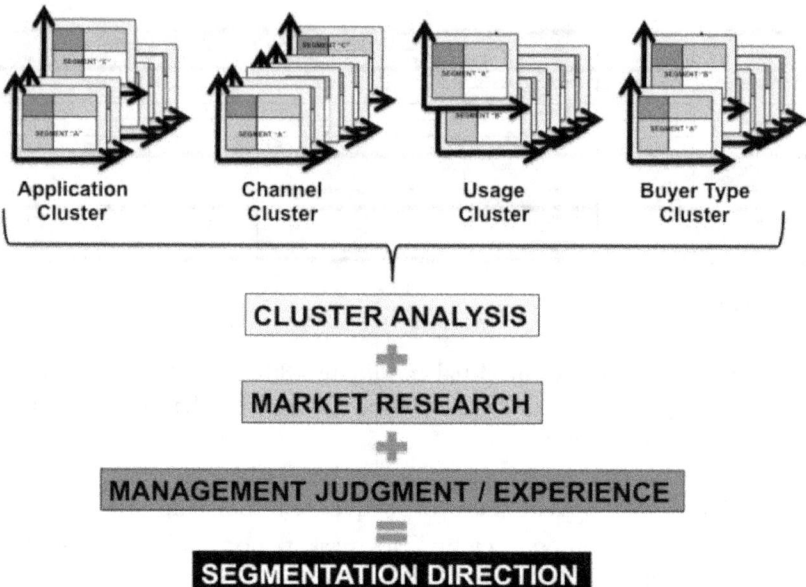

Figure 29.

As shown in figure 29, the analysis looks at the CP matrices within each cluster and compares their respective outcomes (using quad analysis, for example) with other alternatives and with those from the original parent segment. Table 29 gives an idea of the comparison tool based on HDV Brakes example.

| Comparison Criteria | Parent Segment | Application | | | Channel | | Usage | | Buyer Type | |
|---|---|---|---|---|---|---|---|---|---|---|
| | | On-Highway | Specialty | City Bus | OEM | Aftermarket | Light Duty | Heavy Duty | Private | Government |
| Q1 revenue dollars | | | | | | | | | | |
| Q1 contribution margin dollars | | | | | | | | | | |
| Percentage of 80 customers | | | | | | | | | | |
| Percentage of 80 products | | | | | | | | | | |
| Growth opportunity for Q1 | | | | | | | | | | |
| Conversion opportunity from 20 to 80 customers | | | | | | | | | | |
| Optimization opportunity (complexity reduction) | | | | | | | | | | |
| Etc.... | | | | | | | | | | |

Table 29.

In the HDV Brakes example, they initially opted to segment the city bus BU from the overall truck and bus BU. The analytics show a nice margin opportunity to focus on the most profitable customer grouping, which requires a different seller-buyer relationship. Later on, after the validation phase, HDV saw that customers in other groups also felt

136

attracted to the new UVP and decided to adjust their segmentation scope to severe-duty (truck and bus) customers.

Analytics and market research help greatly with the selection of the best segmentation hypothesis, while the validation process will reduce the risk of going forward with the wrong method. But as exemplified in the HDV case, companies have to keep an open mind and be willing to change or enhance their models as they learn from the market. Very rarely segmentation fails to deliver results, and the new BU has to be folded back into the parent segment. Based on my experience with these few cases, there are three key reasons why segmentation fails:

1. A lack of involvement, support, or conviction by the leadership team that market segmentation is a viable growth strategy.

2. A misled assumption that the segments selected really exist in the marketplace (e.g., wrongly assuming that there are distinct behavioral differences among the select customer groups).

3. An exclusive and excessive reliance on analytical methods without enough practical market knowledge, experience, or due diligence, leading to selection of the wrong segments.

## Phase Three: Planning for Segmentation

Once you select a direction to segment the business but before you start making changes, it is important to develop a plan for the customer segmentation and validation phase. Planning creates a baseline for monitoring the evolution of the business using the CP matrix analytics and develops the marketing mix for the new segment using the five Ps (price, product, promotion, place, and people).

The five elements or the five P's of the marketing mix are as follows:

1. Product—the UVP coupled with the portfolio of products or services to be offered to customers in the new segment.

2. Price—target price that accounts for the UVP, competition, and contribution margin goals. Other planning items include price lists, discount levels, financing, and other options.

3. Place—decisions related to the distribution channels to ensure the products or services reach the end user customers. This includes

logistical functions, market coverage, distributors, levels of service, and related concerns.

4. Promotion—the communications and sales of the UVP to existing and prospective customers. These decisions involve advertising, media coverage, and public relations, for example.

5. People—the sales and marketing leadership and staff for the new segment. This deals with the recruitment and development of the right mix of people for the nature of the segment.

Using our HDV Brakes example, Table 30 shows the list of decisions that need to be made by the new Severe-Duty BU in relation to the marketing mix.

| PRODUCT | PRICE | PLACE | PROMOTION | PEOPLE |
|---|---|---|---|---|
| Durability | List prices | Distributors | Messaging | Sales leaders |
| Reliability | Discounts | Market Coverage | Advertising | Sales reps |
| Functionality | Credits | Logistics | Media | Metrics |
| Quality | Financing | Service levels | Public relations | Marketers |
| Branding | | | Literature | Sales admin |
| Packaging | | | Website | Succession |
| Warranty | | | Budget | |
| Support | | | | |
| Training | | | | |

Table 30.

Once the marketing plan is finalized, you will normally see changes in the mix of customers and products; therefore, it is highly advisable to recast the 80/20 CP matrices for both parent company and its BUs. Depending on the criteria adopted, the adjusted matrices will show very different characteristics from the original CP matrix, pointing to new optimization opportunities. This should be expected, since you are segmenting the customer base and looking at the market through the lens of a more specialized filter, causing customers and products to shift quadrants versus the original matrix. If the segmentation hypothesis is confirmed, you can expect that at least one of the new segments will require further optimization using the 80/20 tools.

The segmentation hypothesis needs to be tested prior to splitting the existing BUs into new ones, because it is not possible to know right away if the segmentation will fail or succeed. In most cases, it will take months, and in many cases, it will take more than a year before conclusions can be drawn. Regardless, the only way to test the hypothesis is to put it to work in the real market in such a way that you can learn something from the process and protect the business irrespective of the outcome. In fact, the trial and error method is how the BUs evolve in many areas, including innovation and segmentation.

The idea behind the testing is to exercise the segments with an intense focus on the selected customer groupings and attention to the primary reasons that led to segmentation. Only after a trial period of using the customer and portfolio optimization methodologies from the analytics phase (chapter 4) should the business start moving to the other phases of segmentation, which involve more physical separation measures. Figure 30 shows the entire segmentation process under the 80/20 methodology side-by-side with the implementation cycle. Once the segmentation strategy is deemed successful, the BUs can start the process of physical separation of production and warehousing facilities as well as administrative areas. The innovation areas are commonly kept joined until the new BU grows to a size and scope that requires its own innovation center. More discussion on the innovation approach will be provided when I discuss evolution and innovation in chapter 7.

### Segmentation and hypothesis validation:

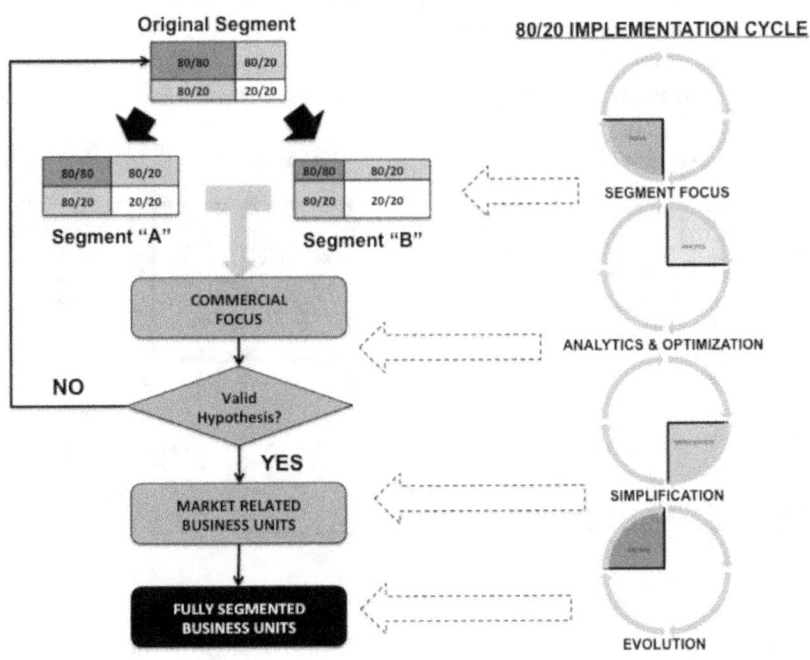

Figure 30.

## Phase Four: Commercial Segmentation and Validation

The commercial segmentation, also known as soft segmentation, has two objectives: (1) to validate the segmentation hypothesis and (2) to learn from the increased familiarity with the selected customer groups. At this point, the BU will only split the original customer organization system (sales, marketing, and customer support) in two. All other functions in the BUs are kept intact and will continue to provide support to both newly formed segment-focused BUs. In some cases, the BU will opt to reinforce each new organization with a few additional resources to compensate for the increased focus and consequent added sales targets. It is important to assign a leader or a manager to each new customer segment.

The key performance indicators for the commercial segments in phase one are based on revenue growth and contribution margins (the total amount in dollars and in percentage of sales). Under the direct cost method, the variable cost and the contribution margins will be known for each SKU, without any arbitrary allocation to each segment. Period costs and SG&A are also not generally distributed to segments during this phase of the process. The original BU continues to be measured on total profit and loss and free cash flow during phase one. Figure 31 shows a representation of the financial metrics for this phase.

### Financial metrics during commercial segmentation:

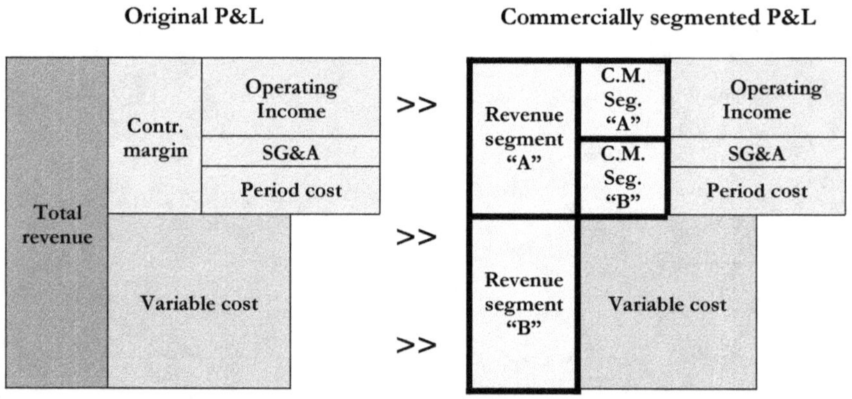

Figure 31.

BUs undergoing segmentation should use a slightly modified metrics management framework to allow for performance monitoring of the customer segments. The types of metrics that should be constantly reviewed in meetings between the BU general manager and the commercial segment managers is as follows:

-Financial metrics (sales, contribution margins, and receivables)
-Changes in the 80/20 CP matrix for the segment
-Absolute sales and contribution margin dollar growth
-UVP sales and margin performance
-Customer feedback and issues

When you are ready to compare the growth and profitability results with your original segmentation goals, there are three possible outcomes from this phase:

1. Segmentation hypothesis is validated—move on to next phase and physically separate the business into two new units (full segmentation). The customer organizations remain intact.

2. Segmentation hypothesis is not validated—reasons for segmentation failure are clear. The customer organizations are merged into one and the original BU stays intact.

3. Results are inconclusive—segmentation has not failed, but the results are below expectations. In most cases, there are clear benefits for continuing with a commercial segmentation focus and remaining in phase one for a longer period of time or until segmentation is revisited.

## Phase Five: Full Segmentation into Market-Focused BUs

Once there is a high level of confidence in the viability of the new segment, the business starts moving into the physical separation phase. This phase can take some time, depending on the complexity of the task; therefore, the planning should be developed to minimize complexity and ensure no disruptions to the business during execution. Figure 32 depicts the move from commercial (soft) to full-blown (hard) segmentation.

## Moving to fully segmented BUs:

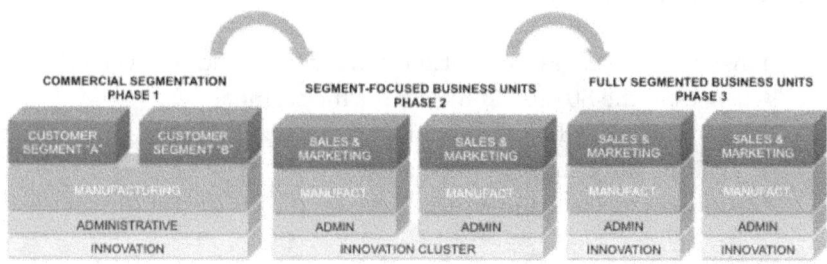

Figure 32.

A helpful tool to kick off complete segmentation planning is called the Business Model Canvas (BMC), which was developed by Alexander Osterwalder.[xxxi] An example of the BMC template is show in figure 33. It's a practical template for developing new or documenting existing BUs based on a visual chart with elements describing the BU's UVP, infrastructure, customers, target segments, and financials.

### The Business Model Canvas (BMC):

| Key Partners | Key Activities | Unique Value Proposition | Customer Relationships | Customer Segment Focus |
|---|---|---|---|---|
| | Key Resources | | Channels | |
| Cost Structure | | | Revenue Streams | |

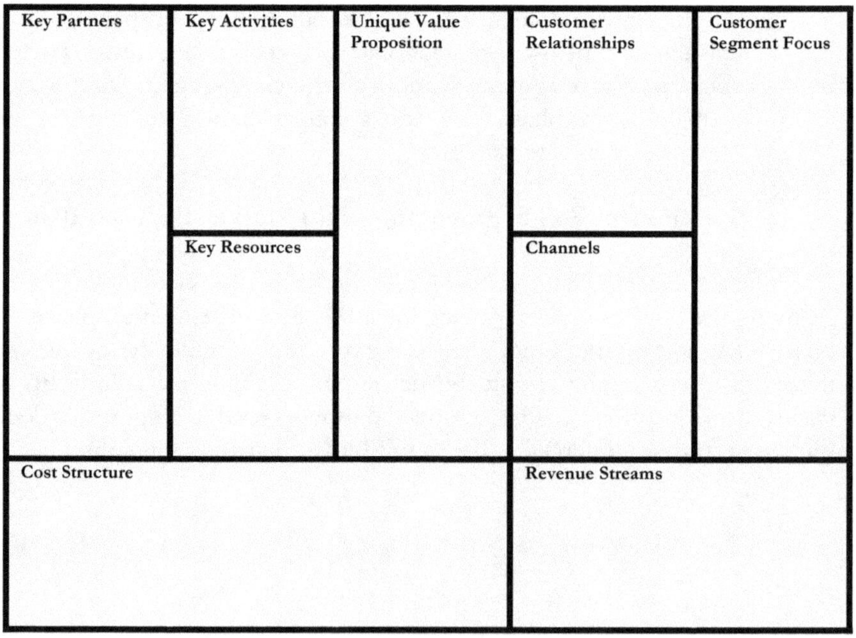

Figure 33.

The key elements in the template are as follows:

- UVPs are what is unique and appealing about the business to the target market (also called singularities).
- Customer segments are clearly identifiable based on the tools and discussions in this chapter.
- Channels are the paths to market that get the UVP all the way to end-users.
- Customer relationships are the types of differentiated services and support that will be provided to "eighty" customers.
- Key activities are the vital few things the BU has to do to deliver the UVP to customers.
- Key resources are the types and quantities of resources to create value to "eighty" customers.
- Key partners are key supplier and distributor relationships.
- Cost structures are the key financial impacts for operating under the new business model. For example, expect an impact from longer product warranties.
- Revenue streams are the way the BU will generate revenue from the customer segment. For example, licensing fees, asset sales, etc.

The BMC tool in figure 33 is especially valuable when creating a new business, during the planning stage, since it allows managers to define the business model in a simple and visual way, for communication and discussion purposes. BMC helps organize all the elements required for a new BU and encourages thinking about key decisions that precede the formation of a full-fledged market-focused segment. Such decisions include:

- Leadership decisions—decide who will take on a general management role for the new BU.
- Planning decisions—determine operating plans and performance expectations over time. How the new BU will be separate from its parent business over time. Zero-based budgeting for parent and child units. Project management and milestones.
- Staffing decisions (beyond sales and marketing)—decide who goes where, whether there are enough people at each BU for it to be functional, what needs to be added, and whether some functions will be shared or centralize for some time.
- Resource decisions—discuss how existing equipment and facilities will be divided between the two new BUs, what else needs to be invested, and how fast these decisions need to happen.

- Operational decisions—decide how the common "twenty" or low-volume SKUs that are common for both BUs should be treated, whether there should be a "feeder low-volume operation" for the "twenty" to serve both units, and whether there is a common sourcing approach.
- Innovation decisions—determine whether to keep one common innovation center, whether the UVP is unique enough that it requires a separate innovation center for each BU, and whether separation of these resources is justified at this stage.

Once the planning starts, there is a natural tendency for the team to want to keep things as they are (or to slow down the pace) and not to provide each BU with dedicated people and assets. I call this separation anxiety, and it is fueled by the fear of adding costs and not harvesting synergies. There will be naysayers at this stage as well; I've seen this happen even when commercial segmentation has proven to be very successful. These fears should be addressed with the ultimate vision about the future state of the business. At this stage, leadership support and involvement from the divisional and corporate levels is critical.

The pace of investment in the new BU is determined by how fast the project can be implemented while keeping the business going and by the amount of resources dedicated to the project. Applying 80/20 thinking to allocate the investment based on a bootstrapping mind-set (as exemplified in chapter 2, bullet number 2) is important. The planning needs to be done in such a way that the new BU can continue to source products from the parent business throughout the entire process.

Whenever companies are splitting BUs, there is an opportunity to remove complexity cost from the parent unit and to build the new BU in the leanest way possible. The tool normally used to remove extra cost is zero-based budgeting (ZBB). Investopedia defines ZBB as "a method of budgeting in which all expenses must be justified for each new period. Zero-based budgeting starts from a 'zero base' and every function within an organization is analyzed for its needs and costs. Budgets are then built around what is needed for the upcoming period, regardless of whether the budget is higher or lower than the previous one. ZBB allows top-level strategic goals to be implemented into the budgeting process by tying them to specific functional areas of the organization, where costs can be first grouped, then measured against previous results and current expectations."[xxxii]

Managers take a deep dive into the parent BU overhead, which is made of the total period costs and SG&A expenses. They use 80/20 thinking to prioritize the expense categories based on their importance levels and visualize the overhead tower—the threshold expenses that are high, medium, and low priorities. Threshold expenses are those mandatory costs to operate the business, such as legal and compliance costs. The remaining expenses are ranked in terms of their added value to the business. In order to have better granularity in this exercise, I recommend that each department develop its own overhead tower before consolidation and action plan development by the segmentation team take place.

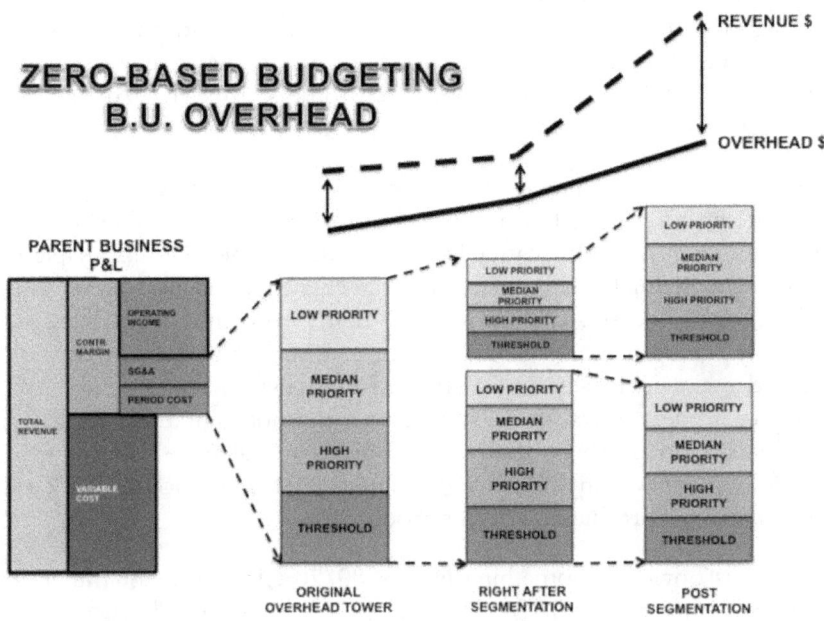

Figure 34.

Figure 34 depicts the ZBB process starting with the parent BU. Once the ZBB exercise is finalized for the parent and the new BU, it is not unusual to see a 5 to 10 percent dollar increase (or sometimes more) in total overhead compared to the original overhead tower. This is expected based on the need to add some additional resources, mainly in support of the newly formed BU. As long as there are still healthy overhead-to-sales ratios for the two units, that should not be a major concern since, in almost every case, the revenue growth quickly brings the overhead ratio below what it was in the original BU.

## Segment-Focused Sales and Marketing

The unique traits of 80/20 in sales and marketing can be summed up in the maxim "some customers are more equal than others." Shuffled among your "eighty" customers are those who buy more frequently and those who are significantly more profitable to the company. This is largely because they value your UVP in different ways, which are maybe not even completely understood by your business. Your UVP is probably helping the customers be more profitable. The economic benefits of focusing sales and marketing efforts on "eighty" customers, both existing and potential ones, should be very clear by now. Not to mention the perverse side of 80/20: spending too much effort on "twenty" customers (the trivial many) will actually detract from your prosperity and even destroy value.

Segmenting the business is the surest way to guarantee you focus on a portion of the market that is more likely to place a higher value on your products and services. No matter how small the segment, the principle of imbalance and inequality still exists; thus, the challenge for the new BU is to find the best customers—the ones with "eighty" potential from sales and profitability standpoints. At the same time, it is important that the new BU create and maintain loyalty among the existing customer base, mainly the vital few customers. Loyalty and steadiness are fundamental for the BU at an early stage. So much so that the BU needs to calculate the monetary value of loyalty from the "eighty" customers and continuously track the frequency and the profitability of this group.

There is obviously something like an 80/20 CP matrix for the entire market segment of the new BU. You probably don't, but if you do have access to all the bits and pieces to complete the analytics, you should build one. But even without the complete market matrix, you need to have an idea about key customers, products, competitors, margins, etc. The finer the segmentation, the better an idea you should have. With this basic information at hand, the BU will compare its CP matrix with the one from the market and identify opportunities such as these:

-Conquest "eighty"—there are probably large potential customer groups out there that are not currently buying from your company. At the same time, products and services could exist in the market "eighty" that are being offered to your customers but that are not in your current portfolio.

-Sleeper "eighty"—sleepers are currently in your list of "twenty" customers and products; however, they are large enough to be considered "eighty" customers by the market. For some reason, they kept a low profile with your company, and you should understand why. You might have a relationship issue with a sleeper customer, or they simply like the competitor's UVP better. On the product side, you may have issues related to price, cost, performance, or a combination of issues.

In his book *80/20 Sales and Marketing*, Perry Marshall describes how to use 80/20 principles to identify the most likely customers that will pay more for your UVP.[xxxiii] He describes an interesting idea in chapter 2 called "rack the shotgun" to illustrate the point that you should spend time up front zeroing in on the customers who are most profitable to your business. Along the same lines, you should devise ways to identify the cons, or those customers that will probably not be in the "eighty." The more clearly you articulate and communicate your UVP to the segment, the better are your chances of identifying the "eighty" prospects.

Perry Marshall goes on to provide helpful ideas to mine for the "eighty" customers using techniques that may look obvious but are often overlooked by companies. Look up your sales data and apply the R-F-M rule—customers that bought most recently, bought most frequently, and spent the most money. Pinpoint your "eighty" customers on a map and see whether you find clusters or geographical patterns. Look for additional niches within your market segment. Now that you have zoomed into a new cluster with segmentation, you can reapply 80/20 analytics in many different ways and discover patterns that were hidden before.

Regarding products and services, even after you've applied all the simplification tools from 80/20 and separated the high-volume from the low-volume products, there is still a level of customization left in every portfolio that may very well be an important component of your company's UVP. There is always an opportunity to become a smart customizer for your "eighty" customers without allowing too much complexity to creep back into the business.

The positives of tailoring the business without all the complexity are expressed in an article by Booz and Company called "Smart Customization" about how to identify virtuous variety that can work for you: "The way a company responds to demands for customized products or services can make the difference between performance that leads a sector and performance that lags that of industry peers…Companies that more effectively balance the value that customization brings to their customers with the complexity costs it can impose generate organic sales growth and profit margins significantly higher than their industry average."xxxiv

The benefits come from several elements:

1.  Understand sources of value from customization—find out what your portfolio currently has that is different from the competition's and understand how the "eighty" customers value it.

2.  Focus on the right customization strategy—use the Kano model (explained in chapter 7) to distinguish between basic needs, performance needs, and delighters.

3.  Tailor business streams to provide value at the least cost—better align your delivery model with needs that differentiate performance for key segments, and redesign key processes to meet needs while reducing the overall cost to serve. "Smart customizers match their segmentation strategies with delivery mechanisms design specifically to serve each segment profitably."

During the analytics and optimization phase of the 80/20 process, I've talked about several ways to differentiate commercial policies and levels of service between "eighty" and "twenty" customers. However, it is not unusual for companies to apply a certain level of smart customization among their "eighty" customers, since they all have different needs. But here again, companies need to focus on the right type of customization that is in most cases already built into the UVP. In the HDV Brakes example, we can see how each major customer will require different levels of training and support to customize its brakes. A specialty logging (forestry) truck may need slightly different parts in its repair kit than a public utility truck, for example.

When it comes to the "eighty" customers, your sales and marketing teams must have a credible and genuine sense of ownership for them. Their attitude toward the customers is everything since every contact with the company is an opportunity to strengthen or weaken the relationship. The vital few customers must be regarded as assets of the BUs, very much like plants and buildings are. Always remember that these customers represent 80 percent of your revenues and profits. Instead of throwing money away on old-fashioned customer surveys, use innovation tools to uncover customer needs and pain points. Frequently talk with your "eighty" customers face-to-face, and walk in their shoes for a while. Making them into loyal and steady extensions of the business is the ultimate goal of the organization. Over time, loyalty and steadiness will reduce the cost to serve them and improve both customer and employee retention rates.

Beyond sales, every interaction between someone from the business and a customer has an impact on the relationship for better or for worse. Companies can use these opportunities to gently remind customers why they choose the company's products. There is always more happening in a transaction than just an exchange of a product or a service, such as accurate and prompt information, documentation, delivery promises, and many other things. Trying to satisfy the customer with only a product or a service is not going to be sufficient. A problem with one of the elements of the value package that happens during the so-called moment of truth can compromise the relationship with an "eighty" customer.

Be prepared to invest in relationship building with "eighty" customers. You need to be more than a vendor. Become a reliable source of information and support. Be a consultant when customers need a problem solved, even if it is not directly related to your product lines. Spend time with them outside the business setting. Organize events and fun activities to do with your "eighty" customers, if possible—fishing trips, golf outings, and related activities will allow you to get to know each other personally. After spending personal time with an "eighty" customer, it's hard to think of any problem that cannot be solved in a more natural way.

Finally, to retain customers, you should work hard to retain your best employees. Employee turnover is one of the biggest hurdles to building customer loyalty. Steady and satisfied employees will not only be more productive, but they will have a much better understanding of what it takes to keep a customer coming back. They will become more proficient at resolving customer problems and at finding pain points, turning into a consistent source for innovation and continuous improvement.

Satisfying employees is not all about compensation. The "eighty" employees like to be in an independent BU and need to be empowered, listened to, and provided with a working environment that has an entrepreneurial flavor to it. They embrace accountability and act responsibly. If you want to have loyal customers, think about creating loyalty within the employees of the BU while you free them up them to run their own business units.

In summary, segmentation is not just about marketing, but it is mainly about the way you run the business, to focus on the vital few customers, and to grow without adding more complexity. By focusing on segmentation you will be able to specialize your value proposition and deaverage your business, while empowering your best people to succeed.

# CHAPTER 7
# EVOLUTION AND INNOVATION

*Innovation is not the result of thinking differently. It is the result of thinking deliberately (in specific ways) about existing problems and unmet needs.*

*—Anthony W. Ulwick*

The laws of evolution and natural selection principles point to the fact that only an adaptable species will grow and thrive, while the nonadaptive ones shrink and eventually become extinct. Adaptability means effective adjustment to new and unpredictable conditions that appear in the environment. In nature, the species that evolve most effectively use a combination of both defensive and offensive strategies. In other words, you must be prepared to defend your existence by reacting to threats, but you must also be capable of anticipating change and creating new opportunities to enhance your position in the food chain.

In business, you need to be competent to defend your core activities and explore incremental opportunities, but you also need to be capable of developing new strategies that can lead to transformational growth. The key to new strategies is innovation, which is the driving force behind adaptability and the skill that yields direct change. Peter Drucker has a simple, elegant definition for innovation: "Change that creates a new dimension of performance."

There are many types of innovation; however, we will discuss two types with distinct characteristics—incremental and breakthrough. Incremental or applied innovation is present throughout the entire 80/20 implementation cycle, while breakthrough innovation is a deliberate and systematic way to attain transformational growth and to create a type of force field around the core of the business to keep competitors from eroding your profitability. Throughout this book, we will refer to incremental innovation as segment-focused innovation, since it is generated by the BU and focused on a specific market segment. We will also refer to breakthrough innovation as systematic innovation, since this type of innovation needs systemic and consistent effort to occur. Both types of innovation go beyond product invention and innovation.

The force field is analogous to the economic moat expression coined by Warren Buffett—the effectiveness of force fields and moats oscillate and need to be continuously reenergized or refilled to provide adequate protection against "invaders". Figure 35 depicts the fact that innovation is a requirement to expand the business beyond the core. Without innovation and growth the core business will be compromised over time.

**Going beyond the core with different innovation types:**

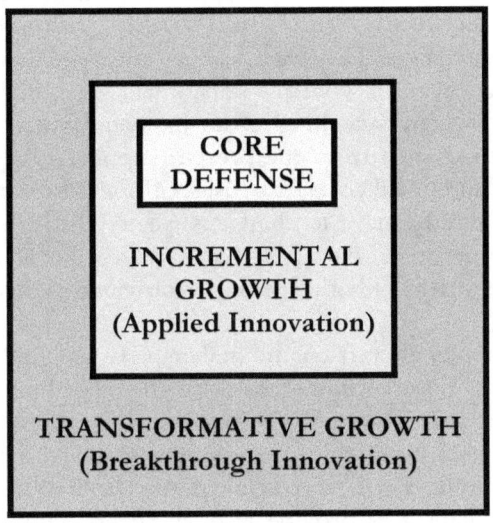

Figure 35.

## The Economic Moat

There is an article from Matt Linderman[xxxv] that explains very well Warren Buffett's belief in economic moats: "When looking to purchase a business, Buffett pays careful attention to a business he understands not just in terms of what the business does but also of what the economics of the industry will be 10 years down the road, and who will be making the money at that point." He is "also looking for enduring competitive advantages." This, in a nutshell, is what makes a company great: the width of the moat around the company's core business.

The economic moat denotes a company's strength level in a certain industry in terms of a sustainable competitive advantage or, even better, a comparative advantage. It can be defined in terms of a palpable and measurable hurdle that keeps competitors from diminishing or destroying the company's leadership position and profitability. At the same time, the moat makes the market structure healthy by imposing barriers for new entrants. To use Buffett's analogy, a large and deep moat surrounding the castle helps to keep the "barbarians" from entering the gates and stealing the valuables inside. The main features of wide moats are as follows (and are illustrated in figure 36):

1.  High switching costs. When there is a significant downside for customers that want to change to a new supplier—such as when the incumbent company differentiates the levels of service and support between "eighty" and "twenty" customers—it creates a barrier to change. The "eighty" customers are given a comparative advantage over the "twenty" customers. The other type of feature related to high switching costs happens when it is painful for buyers to change from the present supplier to a new one, in the form of additional costs, expenses, or one-time inconveniences. An artificial disadvantage to change is created through pain that can be labeled negative costs. In this case, buyers need a large improvement in either price or performance to make the change.

    For example, aircraft engine makers GE and Rolls Royce develop extremely close relationships with their "eighty" customers—the major airlines. They offer differentiated support for maintenance, which makes it difficult for customers to switch between brands, at least without a lot of consideration. In the same industry, the airlines themselves provide frequent flyers with special privileges, such as free upgrades and other perks. Depending on the airline, these privileges range from being a comparative advantage to a negative cost. Airlines have created different customer classes (e.g., diamond, platinum, gold, and silver). At the higher levels where the "eighty" customers are, there is a downside to change from the current airline to a competitor. Examples of negative costs can also be found in the mobile phone industry. Most carriers build in fees and penalties to make it difficult for customers to leave their systems. While this is somewhat successful for carriers, the more sustainable strategies are those from companies that build comparative advantages into their products or services.

2.  Low cost producers. Focus on being a low cost producer, not just on being a low price marketer. Even if you offer a commoditized product, aim at being the best at creating availability at the lowest cost in the industry, all the way from the raw materials supply chain to the production facilities to the distribution channel. This is a weapon to use when competitors try to gain market share by undercutting your prices.

    Dell Computer Corporation is a good example. Its manufacturing and supply chain strategies are geared toward high-volume, low-cost production and channel disintermediation when selling to end users (Dell direct model). It pioneered direct online sales instead of using resellers. Dell has become an expert in pushing high-end data and computer products into this commoditization mode and then producing and delivering them at the lowest cost in the industry. They did this with computer graphic stations and mass data storage devices, which were not considered commodity products at the time.

3.  Network effect. It occurs when the value of a product or service goes up proportionally with the growth of the customer or user base. The more people buy or use something, the more valuable it is. Value can also be enhanced when new features and benefits are released after delivery and adopted by the customers.

    For example, several e-commerce companies benefit from the network effect, especially those who attract large numbers of members that interact with one another. Let's look at eBay, where the very large number of users makes the service extremely valuable and hard to replicate. Another example is American Express, the global credit card company. As the number of users grows, the more accepted and valuable the company gets. The company continuously enhances its services with new features and benefits for cardholders, specializing in subsegments of the broader market such as affluent individuals, small businesses, and corporations. And finally, as of July 2015, Facebook announced at their quarterly earnings call that they have reached the milestone of 1.4 billion members worldwide. More people than the population of China log on to Facebook every day. The network effect of Facebook is propelling the company's value above $250 billion.

4.  Intangible assets. Intangible assets are intellectual property in different forms, such as patents, proprietary processes, and even trade secrets that cannot be easily duplicated by competitors. Strong and well-established brands with high mindshare also constitute valuable assets to attract new and retain existing customers.

For example, companies with many active technology patents, such as Qualcomm, are rich in intangible assets: Its inventions helped launch the mobile revolution and can be found in billions of devices around the world, from smartphones and tablets, to cameras and cars, and beyond. Others have unique processes that provide a comparative advantage. In manufacturing, ITW has in-line manufacturing systems and Toyota has TPS (Toyota Production System). In the area of new product development (NPD), Apple has a unique process called ANPP (Apple new product process) that starts with a heavy focus on design and is developed by dedicated teams as if they are separate start-up companies. Businesses with trade secrets and strong global brands, like Coca-Cola and Gillette, are good examples of how mindshare can become a powerful intangible asset.

**The economic moat:**

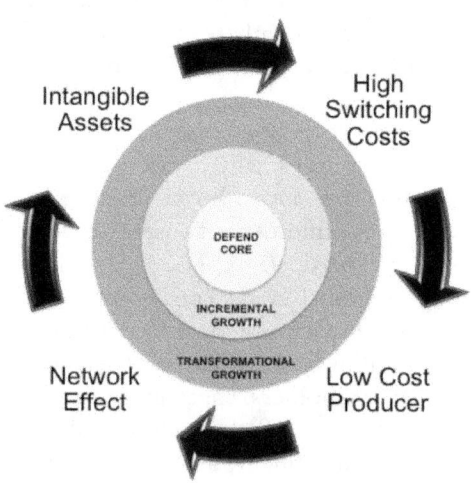

Figure 36.

The fact is that not all features have to be present at the same time in order to provide a wide moat. Most companies with wide moats do not have all features present. The most important trait, however, is to evolve and innovate, in the broader sense of the word innovate, beyond products and past the existing business model design. This evolution requires systematic innovation on multiple dimensions, such as product offerings, manufacturing processes, and customer experiences and in the business model itself. It requires both incremental and breakthrough innovation.

As you look closer, it's no coincidence that the moat's features are aligned with the vital few natural laws and with the 80/20 implementation cycle (see table 31).

| MOAT FEATURE | NATURAL LAW | 80/20 TOOLS |
|---|---|---|
| High switching costs | Vital few and trivial many | Develops a strong bond with "eighty" customers so they remain loyal. |
| Low cost producer | Simplicity | Assigns lowest cost production lines to "eighty" products through PLS and BPS. |
| Network effect | Fractal behavior | Focuses closely on market segments and specialization. |
| Intangible assets | Evolution | Uses incremental and breakthrough innovation. |

Table 31.

Companies usually have processes in place for delivering on incremental growth, such as new product development (NPD) and concept-to-customer tools, in order to defend their core businesses and enter similar or adjacent markets. However, breakthrough innovation requires a new approach to innovation that goes beyond product invention and past entering adjacent markets. These true needle-moving innovation strategies are required to create unbreachable moats.

## The Two Innovation Categories

To succeed in developing a sustainable innovation strategy, we need to work on two different and complementary areas: The first is driven by the BUs or the market segments and focuses on product portfolio and market-segment needs. The other is driven at the company level, using a system-wide, multidimensional process (beyond products) and involving different segments that are highly connected with the strategic company roadmap. The two categories of innovation are as follows:

1. Segment-focused innovation (SFI) is also known as incremental or applied innovation. This type of innovation is driven by the BU and its primary purpose is to defend the business core and find incremental growth. It innovates primarily by solving problems for customers and markets.

   The SFI process starts with a complete understanding of the problems or pain points faced by the "eighty" customers within a specific market segment, and via ideation and problem solving methodologies, the pain points are converted into ideas and solutions. Market-segment-focused business units are better prepared than any other type of organization to find the market pain points and deliver innovative solutions to known and unknown customer problems. These BUs are closer to end users and use innovation to attain incremental growth and profitability. SFI can be described as an empirical path, because it is highly dependent on trial and error. BUs need the freedom to experiment with many ideas, since not of all them will work. SFI creates a sharp and unique view of the market segment using 80/20 analytics as a powerful microscope to slice and dice the customer base and the problems faced by the market. This is where the majority of product and service innovation in the business world comes from— listening to customers and figuring out how to solve the pain points of the market in a collaborative way.

   Although SFI can be very effective and productive, in almost every case it creates solutions and ideas geared toward defending the core business and generating incremental revenues and profits. Unless there is a flash of genius, the empirical process rarely lends itself well to creating breakthrough ideas and transformational growth. A deliberate, proactive, and consistent innovation process, driven by the top leaders of the organization, with strategic goals in mind, is a superior way to create transformational growth and a sustainable moat. This approach is called systematic innovation (SI), and it consists of a methodical process to examine a larger number of dimensions in a multidisciplinary way, converging on an optimal solution.

2. Systematic innovation (SI) is also known as breakthrough innovation. This process is driven by the company's senior leadership with multidisciplinary teams, in order to pursue transformational growth. SI links innovation with the company's strategic goals or strategic ambitions, anticipating market needs for new business model designs.

SI starts with the strategic goals from multiple BUs and with the strategic ambition or intent from the top of the company. SI then applies innovation tools to converge these goals and ambitions into the vital few strategic initiatives that aim to transform the company. The reason we need both segment-focused and systematic innovation is because we cannot afford to leave evolution and moat creation at the mercy of someone in the organization who has a flash of genius. While it is very possible to have thought leaders and innovators within the organization who come up with these ideas from time to time, this should not be the primary source for innovation. To succeed in both types, you must use discipline, methods, and perspiration. Innovation workshops that are as frequent as business reviews, and a healthy pipeline of pain points and needs, are key requirements to deliver breakthrough innovation.

As Clayton Christensen points out in his two brilliant books The Innovator's Dilemma[xxxvi] and The Innovator's Solution,[xxxvii] companies can put too much focus on what they are able to read in the markets today. They can neglect to anticipate areas of future customer needs, both in terms of products and business model designs. Christensen uses the expression "disruptive innovation" to describe changes to business models that are capable of creating new markets and value networks, displacing earlier technologies. Systematic innovation drives the consistency and the discipline necessary to innovate in different dimensions in order to keep up with the technology and to evolve the business model, reducing the likelihood of being displaced by disruptive innovation coming from existing competitors or new entrants.

Improving on the business model and transcending invention does not necessarily require new technologies or the creation of new markets. In a *Harvard Business Review* article entitled "Four Paths to Business Model Innovation," Karan Girotra and Sergei Netessine propose that innovations to the business model are actually changes to the following decisions: "What your offering will be, when decisions are made, who makes them, and why. Successful changes along these dimensions improve the company's combination of revenue, costs, and risks."[xxxviii] In other words, they propose that companies should sharpen their focuses and recalibrate their mixes of products or services to find the sweet spot.

When companies combine segment-focused strategies with systematic innovation using 80/20 analytics, they arrive at optimal product and service mixes that offer the greatest potential for innovation and transformational growth. They also derive better pictures of their markets and customers that will benefit from the changes to the business model. Next I will cover the different innovation dimensions and explain the processes for attaining both segment-focused and systematic innovation.

## Segment-Focused Innovation

This innovation category is sponsored by the BU and directed to a specific segment of the market. Although 80/20 analytics are built around customers and products, the types of innovation we see from this process can go beyond markets and product offerings into areas such as manufacturing processes, distribution channels, finance operations, and overall business models. Throughout the 80/20 implementation cycle, there are many opportunities for innovating:

1. Analytics phase—innovation can arise from portfolio optimization, including changes to business practices associated with "eighty" and "twenty" customers.

2. Simplification phase—product architecture can change using PLS (product line simplification), simplification of business processes, and in-lining, which can create production process innovation.

3. Segmentation phase—new approaches to BU management and to innovation in fractal segments for the "eighty" customer base can provide specialized solutions.

4. Growth phase—multiple ways to attain sustainable growth and to develop relevant innovation on business design strategies can help a company grow.

The challenge is to identify innovation strategies that deliver uncommon advantages. Here we can resort back to 80/20 analytics to help us decide which strategies to use, bearing in mind that the current CP matrix may not completely represent the ideal or desirable state, as you may find there are "twenty" customers and products that are targeted to become future "eighty" customers and products someday. Still, start with what you have today and use a data-based approach to decide.

**Innovation strategies derived from the CP matrix:**

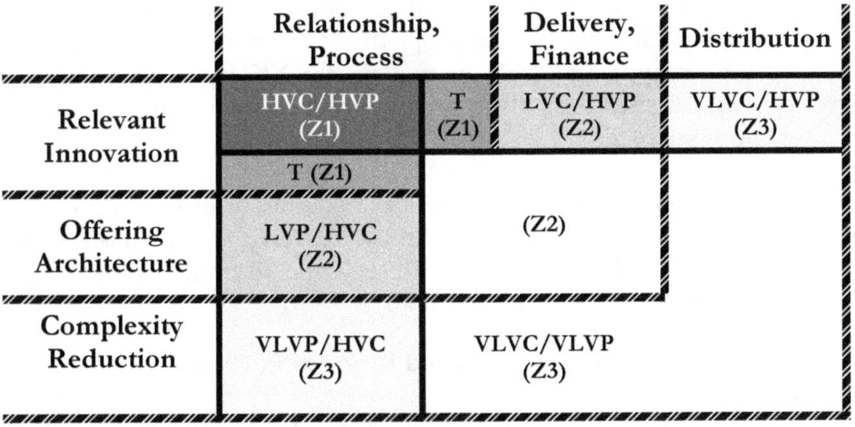

| | Relationship, Process | | Delivery, Finance | Distribution |
|---|---|---|---|---|
| **Relevant Innovation** | HVC/HVP (Z1) | T (Z1) | LVC/HVP (Z2) | VLVC/HVP (Z3) |
| | T (Z1) | | | |
| **Offering Architecture** | LVP/HVC (Z2) | | (Z2) | |
| **Complexity Reduction** | VLVP/HVC (Z3) | | VLVC/VLVP (Z3) | |

Figure 37.

In figure 37, the y-axis defines the nature of the product innovation. As you move from top to bottom, innovation becomes less strategic and more tactical and operational. The x-axis shows the nature of innovation applied to the business model, again from strategic to tactical to operational, as it moves from "eighty" to "twenty" customers. If we look at the three zones in the matrix, we can define the different requirements for innovation:

-Zone 1 requires relevant innovation, which touches almost all aspects of the business including products, processes, and customer relationship management. Relevant innovation should be executed with the objective of creating a sustainable comparative advantage for the company and for its "eighty" customers. Typical approaches here are significant process improvement (e.g., in-lining) and resolving important business problems for "eighty" customers.

-Zone 2 requires tactical innovation, which invests just enough resources to optimize the portfolio and reduce complexity costs. Most of the innovation in this zone comes from PLS (product line simplification) and changes to processes that impact "twenty" customers. The typical outcome is a redesigned portfolio with significantly fewer SKUs (by combining, replacing, and substituting), a plan to outsource to expert suppliers, different lead times, etc.

-Zone 3 requires hygienic innovation, which is focused on cleaning up clutter and charging appropriately for transaction complexity. Typical approaches are pricing up the SKUs, rechanneling low-volume customers, discontinuing products, and firing customers if necessary.

SFI focus and resource allocation needs should be driven by the 80/20 rule, based on the analytics. If we are to defend the core business and sustain growth in the market segment, we need to create innovation for customers and products in quadrant one.

## The Segment-Focused Innovation Process

The innovation process within a specific market segment is divided into five sequential steps (shown in figure 38).

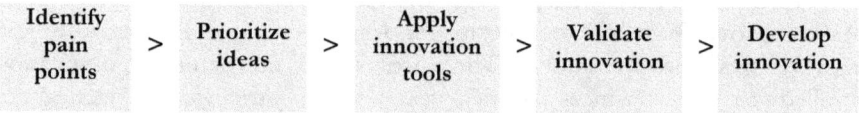

Figure 38.

## Step One: Identifying Pain Points

The first step in segment-focused innovation is to find the customer's or market's pain points. Before going to the market in search of pain points, it's important to select the customer segment(s) you will focus on. Start with your "eighty" customers and products in zone one and break them into a few clusters or subsegments.

Finer segmentation will help you maintain sharp focus when discovering pain points. Segments will vary according to the nature of the products or services in your portfolio. Here are some typical segments that you may develop:

-Customer groupings may be broken down by location, marketplace, industry, or organization type or by buying patterns, duty cycles (how they use the product), etc.

-Product groupings may be determined by application, functionality, price tag, contribution margin level, complexity, number of components, where they are made, etc.

-The key to attaining relevant innovation using SFI is to identify what customers will buy before the products or services even exist. Almost no one could tell you that they needed an electronic spreadsheet before Dan Bricklin and Bob Frankston introduced VisiCalc in 1978. Nowadays we can hardly do any office work without an Excel spreadsheet. The fact is, people were in pain doing manual calculations, but they did not know what could eliminate the pain. People will pay for innovation that eliminates or reduces their pain points, and they will also pay for products that bring pleasure or offer them a better future. So it's essential to look for those things that cause pain and for situations that people find important to achieve their goals.

Most times pain points are not obvious and fall in the category of unspoken needs. The Kano model (see figure 39) calls these delighters. Until you experience the pain from the customer's perspective, it is hard to understand and articulate the issue. In these cases, you need to look for indications that pain is present, such as discomfort, frustration, lack of productivity, or even lack of profitability. Innovative companies have customized tools to look for pain points and keep a healthy pipeline of ideas going all the time.

There are many helpful tools that can be used to identify pain points for zone one. I will briefly cover a few examples, without exhausting the information for each method since it is widely available.

Use the Kano model:

- The Kano model[xxxix], developed by Professor Noriaki Kano, is a framework for classifying innovation and customer satisfaction. It separates the customer's needs into three attributes:

  • Basic—things that are taken for granted by your customer.

- Performance—things that are directly correlated to achieving customer satisfaction and are used by the customer to evaluate you versus your competitor.
- Delight—unexpected features that address normally unspoken needs.

- Needs will drift over time from delight to performance to basic. The migration from a higher level to a lower one is driven by evolving customer expectations and by the level of performance from competing products or services.

- The Kano model works through one-on-one interviews with "eighty" customers. Use the information you gather to develop a list of features or needs for each of the three attributes of the Kano model.

**The Kano model:**

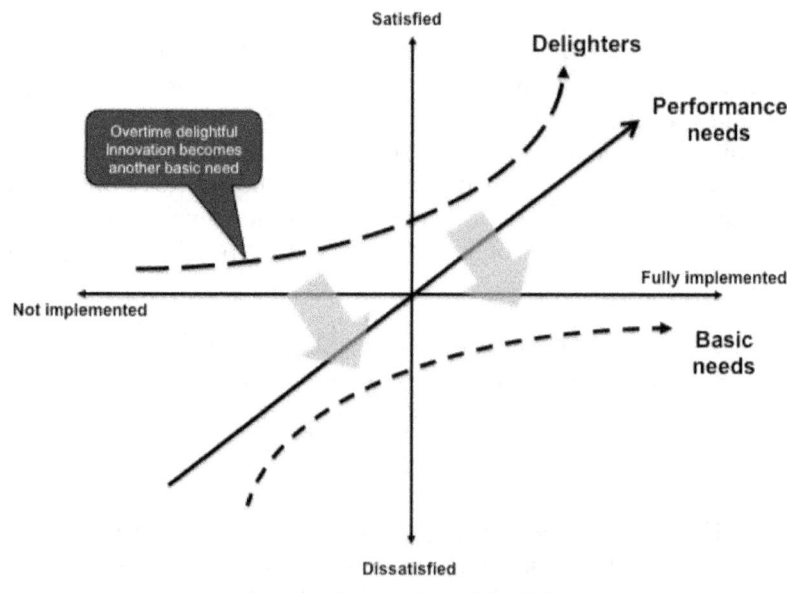

Concept and diagram created by Dr Noriuki Kano

Figure 39.

Take a walk in the "eighty" customer's shoes:

-Experience the world from the perspective of your "eighty" customers. If they are in the transportation business, spend time delivering goods with the drivers or fixing trucks at the service shop. If they are in the retail business, spend time behind the counter. Experience firsthand how your products are actually used by the customer.

Apply the five-why technique[xl] on customers in one-on-one interviews:

- This is a helpful iterative question-asking process used to explore cause and effect for a particular customer problem and to get to its root cause. You simply repeat the question "why" five times in sequence, making sure that each question forms the basis of the next question. Asking five times comes from empirical observation of the number of iterations necessary to get to the root cause.

- Here is an example to get to the root cause of why a car won't start:

    1. Why won't the car start? The battery is dead.
    2. Why? The alternator is not working.
    3. Why? The alternator belt is broken.
    4. Why? The alternator belt was old and worn out.
    5. Why? The vehicle was not maintained properly (the root cause).

List requests from "eighty" customers:

- It is very common for "eighty" customers to have specific requests to solve pain issues or to add new features.
- These requests are golden opportunities to interact with the customers one-on-one and try to obtain answers to the following questions:

    • What problems are they trying to solve?
    • How unique or specific are these problems?
    • What innovations or features will make the most impact for "eighty" customers?

Conduct in-depth interviews with your "eighty" sales and service people:

- Your best sales and service people may know customer's pain points and have ideas to solve them. Whenever you have sales meetings, take the opportunity to organize a separate discussion with a subset of your best people to brainstorm and prioritize pain areas and ideas to solve them.

Review warranty claims and customer support calls:

- Use customer complaints and warranty claims as a source of pain points. Some companies send out service support people to visit with complaining "eighty" customers to learn about the pain caused by a product's lack of performance or failure. Organize periodic meetings with these customer advocates to review the pain points and to come up with solutions.

Benchmark your competitor's "eighty" products:

- Benchmarks and competitive workshops are important tools to determine performance and value gaps versus your key competitors. 80/20 gives you the ability to focus on the vital few products and processes that matter most for the business.

Use ideas from other company areas:

- Promote frequent meetings with team members from sales, service, engineering, and manufacturing to brainstorm areas for improvement, based on the overall experience with customers. Use video and warranty claims, complaints, and customer advocates to stimulate discussion.

### Step Two: Prioritizing Ideas

The second step in segment-focused innovation is to prioritize the ideas you came up with in step one. There are no bad ideas, but not all ideas are equal. The question is how to differentiate between an "eighty" and a "twenty" pain point or customer desire to prioritize the work. I propose that we look at the pedigree of each idea, or in other words, where the idea came from. To do that, we need to consider a series of questions that originates from three different sources of pain points and needs: (1) the direct spoken or unspoken pains and needs from the "eighty" customers, (2) the market and competitive realities, and (3) the company analysis of the market segment. There is no rigid weight scale to attribute scores to each of these questions, but they are generally addressed in this order:

"Eighty" customer experience questions:

- Has the idea originated from a customer?
- Is the idea common to most of the customers you've talked to?
- Does the idea come from walking in the customer's shoes?
- Is the idea considered an unspoken need?
-

Market reality questions:

-Is a solution available in the market?
-Are the customers asking for a different solution?

Internal analysis questions:

-Is the idea a delight attribute in the Kano model?
-Have you applied the five whys to determine the problem's root cause?
-Does the idea appear in the warranty claims or customer service databases?
-Does the idea show up in the customer's requirements list?
-Do the sales and service people recognize the pain or need?
-

After you have answered these questions and decided that your idea is valid, it's time to move on to step three.

## Step Three: Applying Innovation Tools

The third step in segment-focused innovation is to apply innovation tools to your ideas. There are plenty of tools and techniques available for groups to collaborate and generate creative ideas from pain points and customer needs, so I will provide only a small sample based on what has worked most effectively under 80/20. Since there is abundant information available on these tools, I will not spend a lot of time going through the methodology behind each one. Instead, I will try to explain when you should use one type of tool versus another. Innovation tools for group collaboration can be classified in many different ways, but I find these two categories below (divergent and convergent) most helpful to classify the thinking.

Divergent and convergent techniques can be thought of as two different and sequential phases of creative thinking. They complement each other. Divergence is the first phase when you encourage new ideas and stimulate diversity of thought. Intuitive tools, such as brainstorming, are used at this stage, supported by the customer and market information you gathered.

Convergence is the second phase when you focus on finding a solution by refining your ideas and selecting the best ones. Logical and more methodical tools are normally used at this stage, since they use analytical or structured problem solving approaches to get results. An example of a convergent technique is prototyping (also known as pilot trial). Between fanning (divergence) and focusing (convergence), there is room to challenge the possibilities in what I call explore phase (see figure 40).

**Diverge, explore and converge:**

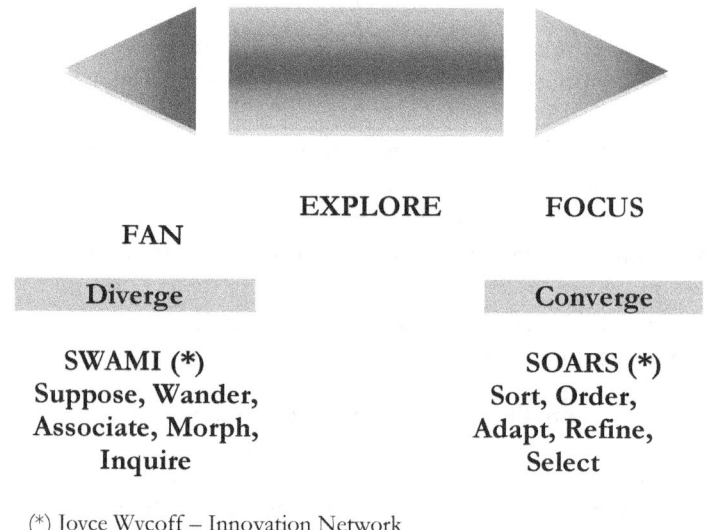

**EXPLORE**      **FOCUS**

**FAN**

**Diverge**                    **Converge**

**SWAMI (*)**                **SOARS (*)**
**Suppose, Wander,**        **Sort, Order,**
**Associate, Morph,**       **Adapt, Refine,**
**Inquire**                  **Select**

(*) Joyce Wycoff – Innovation Network

Figure 40.[xli]

The three phases in figure 40—fan, explore, and focus—are generally used to guide the work on innovation workshops. As far as the techniques to be used for both divergent and convergent phases, figure 41 positions some of the better known tools in each of these two phases, based on the tool nature: intuitive or logical.

**Ideation techniques for innovation workshops:**

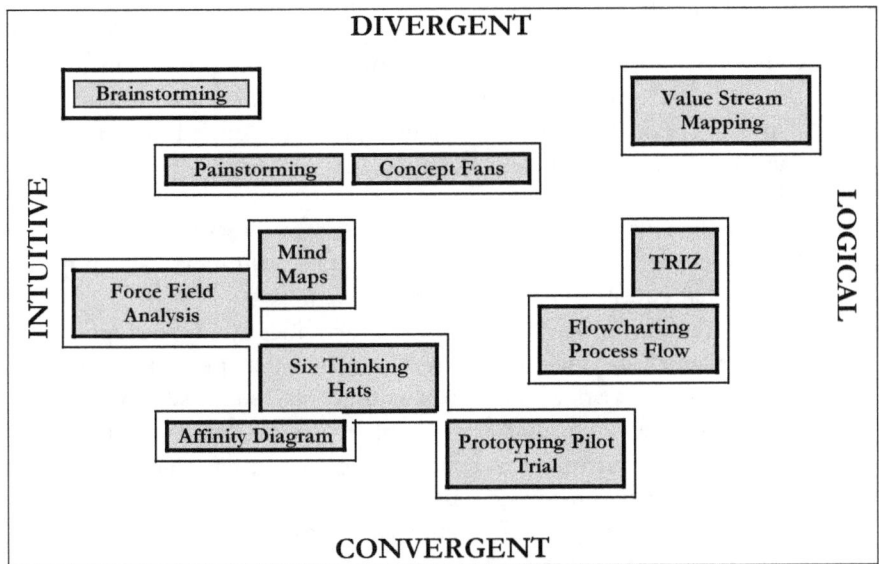

Figure 41.

Most tools do not require prior training, but it is always important to take the time to educate your team before starting an innovation workshop. Other tools, such as TRIZ, require more training and preparation. As your company creates a rhythm of frequent innovation workshops, these tools will come naturally and tend to be adjusted for the peculiarities of each BU.

Brainstorming and painstorming are examples of two widely used tools for the divergence phase. Brainstorming is a technique for groups or individuals to find creative conclusions for specific problems by gathering lists of spontaneously generated ideas. The term was popularized by Alex Osborn in his 1953 book Applied Imagination[xlii]. Osborn claims that groups brainstorming generate ideas more effectively than individuals working alone, although more recent research has questioned this conclusion. Today the term is used as a catchall for all group idea sessions.

In spite of brainstorming's broad use, it's necessary to mention that the effectiveness of pure brainstorming sessions has been questioned recently, since it can be highly subject to group dynamics and psychology. Depending on the group's composition, brainstorming can lead to undesirable biases and to people holding back their ideas. To reduce the probability of failure, I recommend that a facilitator be nominated to moderate the session, allowing for more debate and the presentation of criticisms or counterpoints.

Other less intuitive or more structured methods, like painstorming, can be more effective than brainstorming. Painstorming adds more specificity to brainstorming by asking questions aimed at uncovering customer pain points to drive breakthrough innovation:

-Who is the specific person or customer you're innovating for?
-What are the everyday things that person or customer does? Why, and to what ends?
-What are the processes, tools, or activities that that person or customer does unnecessarily? What has that person or customer invented to work around the way things are supposed to be done?
-What are the root causes of the problems, unmet needs, or desires that person or customer is experiencing? What workarounds is that person or customer using that cause stress, concern, dissatisfaction? Is there anything else responsible for that person's or customer's pain?

Painstorming starts with a situation in mind and identifies the pains associated with that specific situation in order to create a path for opportunity and innovation. Because painstorming in focused on customer problems, it is more likely to generate breakthrough and entrepreneurial ideas when compared to brainstorming.

Now I will address three widely used tools for the convergence phase. Force field analysis is a helpful tool to understand the forces pulling for and against an idea. It especially clarifies how people may oppose or support an idea. The technique requires that you draw a fish bone style diagram, with the objective or desired outcome at the end. On one side, the team lists all the driving forces that have a positive effect on change. On the other side of the diagram, they list the restraining forces that present obstacles for change.

Six thinking hats is another widely used technique created by Edward de Bono[xliii.] It provides good results when you need a team to use different types of thinking. The premise is that the human brain thinks in a number of different ways; participants get to wear different-colored hats to represent each of the six types of thinking or directions—management (the goal), information (the facts), emotion (the intuition), discernment (the risk reduction), optimism (the harmony), and creativity (the investigation). The six thinking hats reveal problems and solutions for an idea from different types of thinking.

The third technique is TRIZ (the theory of inventive problem solving)[xliv]. The acronym comes from Russian—Theoria Resheneyava Isobrethatelskehuh Zadach. TRIZ was developed by G. S. Altshuller and others from the former USSR between 1946 and 1985. It accelerates a project team's ability to solve problems creatively by helping them go back and forth between divergent and convergent thinking based on logic, data, and research. Given the growing importance of this method, I will spend a little more time here to explain the basics.

TRIZ can be thought of as a form of lateral thinking that is based on two universal principles of creativity: First, somebody, sometime, somewhere has already solved your problem or one similar to it. Creativity means finding that solution and adapting it to the current problem. And secondly, don't accept contradictions. Resolve them.

TRIZ research has evolved during the last sixty years and led to other important conclusions:

1. Problems and solutions are repeated across industries and sciences. The classification of the contradictions in each problem predict the creative solutions to that problem.
2. Patterns of technical evolution are repeated across industries and sciences.
3. Creative innovations use scientific effects outside the fields where the innovations were developed.

The TRIZ process consists of applying these findings to the specific situation that confronts you. Figure 42 depicts the process.

**TRIZ problem solving:**

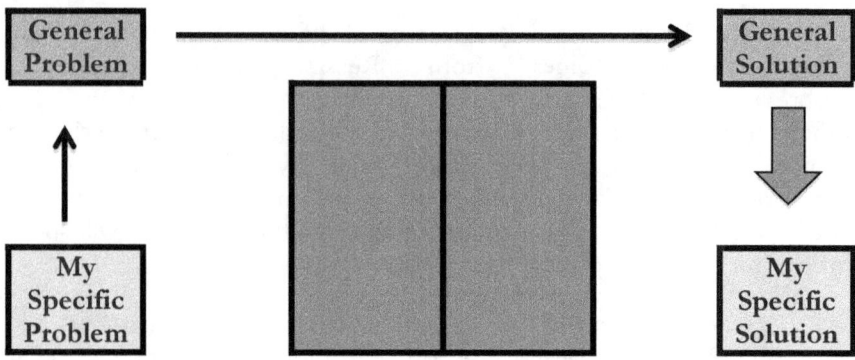

Figure 42.

The arrows in figure 42 represent transformation from one form of the problem or solution to another. The thin arrows represent analysis of the problems and analytic use of TRIZ databases[xlv]. The thick arrow represents thinking by analogy to develop a specific solution. This four-step problem-solving approach forces you to overcome any inherent psychological bias or inertia that typically inhibits intuitive ideation techniques.

As you go into the more specific steps to solve a problem using TRIZ, you will use the following sequence:

1. Identify your specific problem.
2. Formulate the problem (use the prism of TRIZ).
3. Search for previously well-solved problems:
   a. Altshuller extracted a list of thirty-nine standard technical characteristics that cause conflict from over 1.5 million patents worldwide.
   b. These are called the thirty-nine engineering parameters and can be found on the TRIZ40 website.[xlvi]
4. Look for analogous solutions you can adapt to become your solution.
   a. In his research, Altshuller has devised a list of forty TRIZ principles that correspond to a list of known solutions. Studying these existing solutions can inspire you to solve new problems and imagine innovative answers.
   b. The forty principles can also be found at the TRIZ40 website[xlvii].

When selecting the tools you use for your innovation workshops, I suggest you consider the following:

1. Choose more than one technique for the divergence phase of the workshop. Intuitive tools are generally better suited for this portion, depending on the nature of the problem (open or closed). Brainstorming alone, for example has virtues and weaknesses. It is not a bad idea to use more structured tools with brainstorming, like painstorming.

2. Bring data along for the divergence phase. Reports and videos from walking in a customer's shoes, the Kano model lists, and even testimonials from "eighty" customers can greatly improve the efficiency of these tools.

3. Use some time during the explore phase to select the best tool to use during the focus phase. You should consider the nature of the problem (technical or nontechnical), as well as the general background of the people in the room. If the workshop involves resolution of a complex product engineering issue, for example, you will want to use a more technical tool such as TRIZ.

4. Once the tools for the convergence phase have been selected, you have to ensure that everyone has been properly trained and the data and resources have been made available to carry on the focus phase and solve the problem.

### Step Four: Validating Innovation

The fourth step in segment-focused innovation is to validate your innovation from step three. This step involves exposing customers to the new idea early on. In most cases, the BUs develop early prototypes or concept sheets that are shown to customers for an early reaction. Bear in mind that once a team arrives at an idea, they will want to show customers. But they need to consider appropriate intellectual property protection measures, such as early disclosures or pending patents. There are some useful tools to validate your innovation with customers:

- Use focus groups with "eighty" customers:
  - Focus groups are face-to-face meetings with a sampling of your "eighty" customers. They can be used to learn about common pain points at the beginning of the process, but

they are also a well-known method to validate early ideas. They are most helpful when you zoom in on a specific subsegment of customers.

- Focus groups require up front preparation to be successful, such as clear objectives, detailed spec sheets, early prototypes, and thorough frameworks for team interaction with the customers.

- Conduct meetings for user groups:
  - User groups are subsets of "eighty" customers that are focused on a particular product, process, or segment of your business. The advent of online tools makes it easy and convenient for these customers to provide feedback about ideas and pain points all the time.
  - Periodic face-to-face meetings among user groups are also helpful while developing a new product or technology to receive feedback during the actual innovation development phase.

- Hold one-on-one meetings with influential "eighty" customers:
  - Some "eighty" customers have special knowledge about a product or a new process. Granted, you have the idea properly packaged and secured from the intellectual property standpoint, these individual meetings at the customer site can prove very effective to understand the innovation from the customer's point of view.

### Step Five: Developing Innovation

Once the problem has been solved, the next step is to develop the solution. If the solution comes in the form of a product or a new product feature, there are well know methods for ensuring the product is launched reliably, on time and on budget. The complete process from pain identification to launching a new product or a new process is shown in figure 43.

## From ideation to launch:

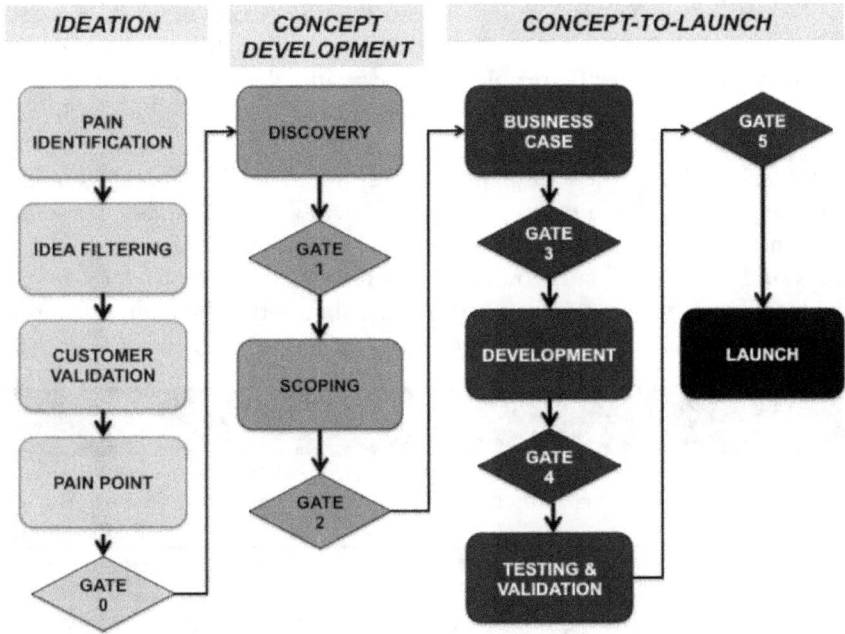

Figure 43.

Note that the main difference between the traditional new product development (NPD) approach and the innovation development process lies at the ideation phase—instead of simply listening to the customer, the business must listen to the market as well and identify both the spoken and the unspoken pain points. The innovation process is therefore opportunistic, driven mostly by how end users act in the market and less by a commercial necessity to sell more of what the company already makes or to fill product gaps with new developments.

Segment-focused innovation anticipates and even influences change in the market; thus, it is necessary to validate ideas with customers before moving forward. In simple terms, segment-focused innovation predicates that one should spend more time up front finding fewer unique ideas from the end user world, instead of filling the pipeline with incremental concepts generated from the inside out.

## The Systematic Innovation Process

What I will call systematic innovation (SI) from now on was also referred to as breakthrough or proactive innovation because you do not necessarily have a specific problem to start with. The general problem is to execute your innovation goals and ambitions in connection with your strategy. There are two main goals for this process: (1) to create value for customers and for the company and (2) to evolve in the direction of building a wide moat in order to sustain growth and profitability in the long run. In order to be proactive, you must become explicit about your innovation ambitions, and you also need to be expansive and look beyond product innovation to attain transformational growth. The main differences between segment-focused and systematic innovation are listed in table 32.

| | SEGMENT-FOCUSED INNOVATION (SFI) | SYSTEMATIC INNOVATION (SI) |
|---|---|---|
| **Nature** | Mostly focused on products and customer segments. | Beyond products and markets into the business model for design innovation. |
| **Sources** | Comes from both customers and company, but more "outside in" than "inside out". | Comes from markets, industry and strategic planning process. |
| **Ideation** | Starts with market pain points and customer needs. | Starts with growth strategy and innovation ambition. |
| **Organization** | Can be managed within the BU or market segments. | Needs a different and protected management structure. |
| **Resources** | Funded by BU P&L and supported by innovation clusters. | Needs separate, protected funds. |
| **Innovation Tools** | Uses divergent and convergent problem-solving tools. | Uses a more expansive framework (ten types of Innovation and twelve vectors). |
| **Metrics** | Uses traditional economic metrics: NPV (net present value), ROI (return on investment), payback and ROS Growth. | Uses long-term economic metrics: growth, ROIC (return on invested capital) and other non-financial indicators. |

Table 32.

Systematic innovation is highly iterative, and it has three distinct stages: (1) finding out what are the right things to pursue (choices), (2) executing and validating the choices (doing it right) and (3) exploring new ways to apply the solution and to leverage the innovation (see figure 44). SI requires several applications of the fan and focus concept, or divergent-convergent thinking, before an idea can be developed and projects can be executed. Starting from the overall company strategy, it distills innovation ambitions into multiple dimensions beyond product invention. After the innovation ambition is clearly articulated, you can consider market realities and set goals, accounting for different segment strategies. These goals define qualitative and quantitative values for your ambition so you know how far you want to go. Only after fully developing the ambition and goals can you move on to creating and selecting a solution prior to the actual development of the idea into a project. The process and the stages can be seen in figure 44.

**The systematic innovation process:**

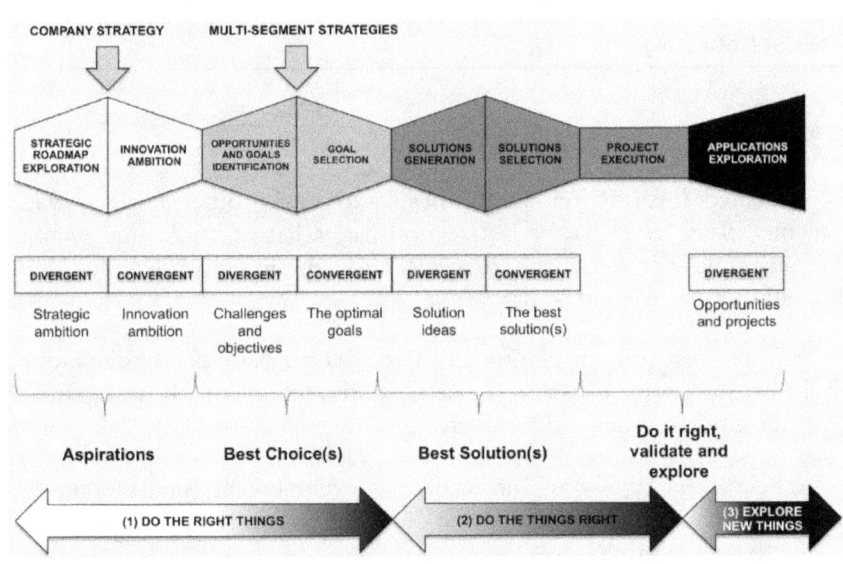

Figure 44.

Several different divergent and convergent tools can be used at each stage of the process, depicted on figure 44. Table 33 is a sampling of commonly used tools for both divergent and convergent thinking, during the first three steps: aspirations, best choice(s) and best solution(s).

**Commonly used SI tools:**

| | DIVERGENT | CONVERGENT |
|---|---|---|
| **Step One: Innovation Ambition (Aspiration)** | - Brainstorming<br>- Concept fans<br>- QFD (quality function deployment)<br>- VOC (voice of the customer) | - Affinity diagram<br>- Six thinking hats<br>- Ten types of innovation |
| **Step Two: Goal Selection (Best choice)** | - Challenge assumptions<br>- Reverse brainstorming<br>- Porter's five forces | - Force field analysis<br>- Twelve vectors |
| **Step Three: Solution Selection (Best Solution)** | - Lateral thinking<br>- SCAMPER<br>- Oblique strategy<br>- TRIZ | - Flowcharting<br>- Process flow<br>- TRIZ |

Table 33.

Detailed information about these and many other tools is widely available. Please refer to the last section for a list of books and websites. One example of a website dedicated to training and learning about innovation tools is MindTools[xlviii].

As we work on stages one and two, selecting areas for innovation, I would like to propose two very useful methodologies to help expand the innovation horizon beyond products:

-The "Ten Types of Innovation" developed by Jay Doblin[xlix]. It proposes a methodology to innovate on different aspects of the business model.

-The innovation radar or the twelve vectors[l] tool developed by Dr. M. Sawhney and Dr. Wolcott from the Kellogg School of Management. The tool proposes innovation directions and helps you benchmark your position versus the market and communicate clearly your innovation strategy to the company.

The ten innovation types can be categorized in different ways, but here I adopt four classes for simplicity—process, offering, delivery, and finance (see table 34).

| CATEGORY | INNOVATION TYPE | DEFINITION |
|---|---|---|
| Process | Enabling process | Enterprise structure, value chain, and partnering |
| | Core process | Proprietary processes that can add value |
| Offering | Product performance | Basic features and functionality |
| | Product system | Extended system that surrounds the offering |
| | Service | How services are offered |
| Delivery | Channel | How offerings are connected to customers |
| | Brand | How an offering's benefits and values are expressed to customers |
| | Customer experience | How an integrated experience is created for customers |
| Finance | Business model | How enterprise makes money |
| | Networking | How enterprise is structure and its value chain |

Table 34.

Successful businesses integrate more than one type of innovation across the company, creating the basis for a powerful moat. As a matter of fact, companies that integrate more than one type of innovation tend to have far superior financial returns in the long term. Table 35 shows examples[li] of companies that innovated in different categories and types using the Doblin model (showing only the key dimension for each company).

| CATEGORY | INNOVATION TYPE | EXAMPLES |
|---|---|---|
| Process | Enabling Process | *Siebel: customer relationship management tools* |
| | Core Process | *GE Capital:* aviation services |
| Offering | Product Performance | *Intel:* Intel Pentium 4 processor performance |
| | Product System | *Microsoft:* Microsoft Office integration architecture |
| | Service | *FedEx:* FedEx range of services and capabilities |
| Delivery | Channel | *NikeTown: innovative approach to retail stores* |
| | Brand | *Virgin:* application throughout products and services |
| | Customer Experience | *Starbucks:* coffee shops becoming hangout areas |
| Finance | Business Model | *Dell:* the Dell Direct Model to reach customers |
| | Networking | *Walmart:* supply-chain model |

Table 35.

As you would expect, not all innovation strategies have the same value according to the 80/20 principle. Doblin researched different types of innovation and their cumulative value creation for a period of ten years for a wide variety of companies in the United States. Although these results correlate with the industry and the nature of each business, less than 2 percent of the projects produced more than 90 percent of the value. At the top of the list of the most impactful types of innovation, you will find business model design and networking, followed by enabling processes and customer experience. At the bottom, you will find categories such as product performance and service offerings. In fact, there are plenty of examples that product innovation alone cannot overcome problems with the business model (e.g., Kodak and Xerox).

The other multidimensional framework that allows you to uncover new types of innovation and benchmark your position versus the market is the innovation radar or the twelve vectors tool.

## The innovation radar (12 vectors):

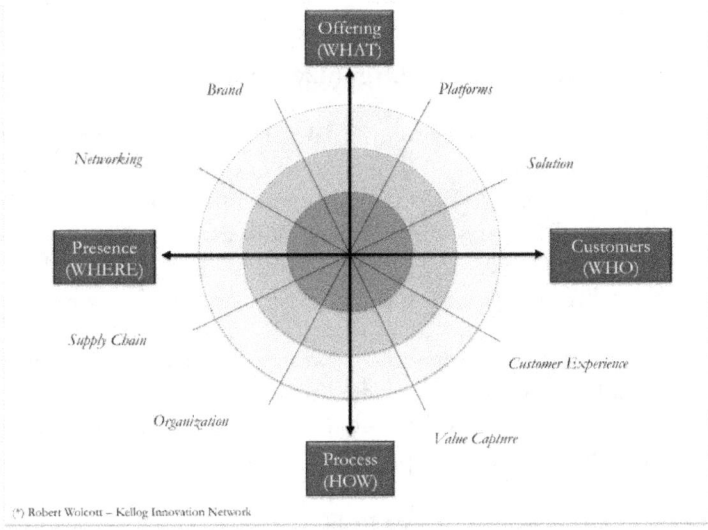

Figure 45.

Companies can innovate along any of the dimensions or vectors in figure 45; however, those companies that tend to focus on two to five vectors tend to do better than companies that try to do a little bit of everything.

The innovation radar has multiple uses in the systematic innovation process. It serves at least four purposes:

- Visualization: track the company's innovation positioning over time
- Benchmarking: show comparative analysis versus other firms in the same industry (or across industries)
- Alignment: communicate and explain a company's innovation strategy
- Brainstorming: explore opportunities for adding new dimensions

Systematic innovation is not a linear process, but the result of multifaceted interactions between individuals, organizations and the environment. It needs innovation-minded leadership, multidisciplinary teams and a large dose of entrepreneurship. SI is critical for the company to survive and thrive in the new economy.

## The Structure and Organization of Innovation

Companies made up of multiple BUs and market segments need to develop proper governance and discipline to execute both SFI and SI. They need organized processes to feed the innovation pipeline with relevant ideas from outside in and to carry on frequent innovation workshops and other specific forums to arrive at valuable solutions. The people leading the processes from different points in the company are the following:

1. The customer advocate(s): they are at the market segment BU level and lead the innovation process from within the BU. The customer advocates are close to the "eighty" customers and are continuously looking for market pain points (pain experts).

2. The chief technical officer (CTO): reside at the innovation cluster. They own the innovation tools, processes, and the labs (such as research and development). They also lead the new product development (NPD) process and supports one or several related BUs.

3. The chief innovation and complexity officer (CCIO): at the senior leadership level of the company, reporting to the chief executive officer (CEO). He or she leads the systematic innovation process for the entire company as well as the complexity management processes.

Innovation clusters or centers are made of people and resources required to carry on segment-focused innovation for one or more BUs. Some large BUs have their own innovation centers. As they segment and grow, the centers end up supporting multiple BUs. There are physical tools (such as testing machines and laboratories) as well as innovation tools and processes that are continuously refined for the needs of the business. The role of the chief technical officer is to provide the means for the BUs to innovate from the outside in. The CTO is also responsible for the new product development process (concept-to-customer).

The chief innovation and complexity officer is a senior leader responsible for creating transformational innovation through the systematic innovation process and tools. The CCIO owns all aspects of the innovation ambition and technology roadmap and leads the work to reduce complexity throughout the company, working with the BU and technical leaders to execute on product line simplification (PLS) and complexity reduction across the board.

Market-segment-focused innovation under an overall company strategy, developed on a systematic framework, is capable of delivering transformational growth and creating a sustainable moat. This framework is called innovation umbrella. Under the umbrella, innovation clusters (or innovation centers) bind related market segment BUs, providing the means, tools, and processes to deliver innovation. The pipeline of ideas is kept constantly full with problems and solutions coming from the bottom, the top and the center of the umbrella. This concept is represented in figure 46.

**The innovation umbrella and additional dimensions of innovation:**

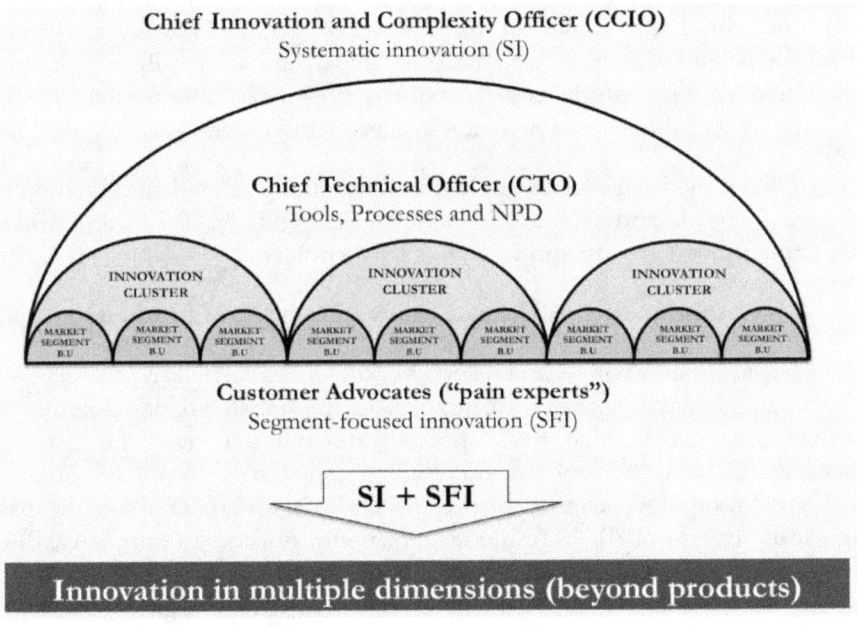

Figure 46.

The innovation umbrella represents the ecosystem to govern the processes within the company. At the base, we have one or more customer advocates per BU. These are people capable of empathizing with customers and bringing the perspective from the market into the company. Normally, we find customer advocates in sales, service, or customer support roles; however, many businesses opt for having dedicated advocates, considering the valuable firsthand customer perspective they bring.

Market-segment BUs conduct monthly innovation workshops in partnership with innovation centers to maintain a healthy flow of pain points and solutions. At a given time, there will be a list of ideas in different stages of execution. In parallel with the segment-focused workshops, the systematic process is carried on with different groups and market segments, working on multiple dimensions of the innovation spectrum. These varied dimensions are clear to the overall organization based on periodic reviews of the innovation ambition and the strategic roadmap.

The outcome of the innovation umbrella is a more diversified portfolio as represented by the framework created by Robert Doblin[lii] and explained by Larry Kelley in his book *Ten Types of Innovation*.[liii] When companies innovate in more than one dimension (normally beyond the invention of new products or services), they have a better chance of creating sustainable value for customers and shareholders.

I will now discuss an example that shows the powerful combination of market-focused and systematic innovation, and how it can deliver transformational growth and value to all stakeholders.

## Cummins Inc.: A Case of Innovation beyond Products

Having started my career and worked for many years at the then Cummins Engine Company, I can attest to the transformational nature of growth and change that has happened at Cummins over the last two decades. In fact, it's one of the leading innovative companies, having delivered way above-average market results to shareholders over the past ten years. In typical 80/20 fashion, ROS (return on sales in terms of EBIT) has grown faster than revenues for Cummins in the last fifteen years. This is a truly remarkable feat for a company that was deemed against the ropes several times during the 1970s and 1980s. The company was locked up in what was once called a failed oligopoly—a reference to the troublesome North American independent diesel engine manufacturing industry, primarily to the on-highway transportation industry.

Cummins was founded in 1919 in the small town of Columbus, Indiana, pioneering the development of diesel engines as a reliable source of power. Today, Cummins is a global power leader with yearly revenues close to $20 billion dollars (circa 2015). It is divided in four major divisions—engines, components, power generation, and distribution. Cummins is present in more than 190 countries and has fifty-five thousand employees worldwide. Each division is composed of multiple BUs. The engine division, for example, is segmented into seven different BUs—heavy-duty truck, medium-duty truck and bus, light-duty automotive and RV, rail, industrial (mining, marine, oil, gas, and government), construction and agriculture, and stationary power.

During the 70s and 80s, Cummins saw increased competition from offshore suppliers—mainly from Japan—and decided against all odds to invest in protecting its core business by launching a new family of midrange engines that became extremely successful around the world. While defending its core businesses, Cummins invested heavily in technology to improve emissions. The rules from the North American EPA and the European agencies have created successive hurdles for engine emissions since 1985, and Cummins used these challenges to focus their innovation efforts. Many times they anticipated what the regulators would do next, increasing the entry barrier for new and established competitors. As a result, other independent engine manufacturers like Caterpillar and Detroit Diesel had to exit the on-highway segment or give up their independence.

During the late 80's and early 90s, concerned with the North American trucking industry's issues and the concept of failed oligopoly, Cummins started to go beyond their comfort zone, investing in new areas such as power generation and components. In the mid-1990s, Cummins created a systematic innovation process to pursue new dimensions and types of innovation beyond product invention. The aim was to improve their business model and reduce their dependence on the on-highway business, making the company less cyclical by default. With a highly committed leadership team, very engaged employees, and a culture of innovation, Cummins was able to innovate in several fronts, at times breaking with old paradigms. Many of today's initiatives originated at that time:

-New business segmentation and focus.
-New technology drives (e.g., electronic controls and components).
-Updated global expansion initiatives (e.g., joint-ventures and acquisitions).
-New distribution business models.
-Improved brand and image.

-Revamped processes (using six sigma tools).

This powerful set of initiatives, driven by excellent people and coupled with an evergreen strategic roadmap, helped create a wide moat for Cummins, primarily in three areas:

-Entry barriers for competitors, high switching costs in emissions technologies, and global partnerships.
-Intangible assets (delivers incremental and systematic innovation).
-Amazing network effects coming from the global footprint and the array of joint-ventures and partnerships, including the distribution network.

Cummins is a prime example of a company that engineered itself to excel at both segment-focused and systematic innovation. These different processes were first embedded in the various management systems of the early 90s (e.g., Cummins production system and Cummins marketing system) and later on adopted under the six sigma umbrella. As it relates to incremental innovation, there are clusters or customer engineering centers in each division, which are similar to innovation centers. Customer engineering organizations not only find new ways to engineer existing products to meet customer needs, but they are also extremely involved in helping segments uncover market pain points by walking in the customer's shoes and using other methodologies. Cummins culture and governance has evolved in such a way that systematic innovation is a way of life, absorbing most of the management team's attention during strategic planning reviews. This is highly encouraging for Cummins, as the best strategies are not only about making choices but also about constantly innovating on the design of the established business model.

# CHAPTER 8
## THE VITAL FEW PEOPLE AND LEADERSHIP

Market-segment-focused BUs are the basic operating entities of companies driven by 80/20 BPI, and effective leaders who can intensely focus on a segment and think in 80/20 ways are at the center of every thriving BU. Once you've identified the vital few people who add the most value to your business, be prepared to work for them, empower them, remove obstacles for them, and give them room to make their own mistakes. The reason for this high level of empowerment and delegation resides in the well-known fact that vital few people create far more value for the business than what they create for themselves. This is not to say that they shouldn't be rewarded generously for the value they create. Quite the opposite—they need to be given substantial compensation for the upside they bring.

When it comes to attracting, developing, or retaining the best individuals, 80/20 companies have a leg up on the competition. They offer unique opportunities for people to run businesses autonomously and manage P&Ls. This is another important consequence of segmentation: great managers have interesting places to go instead of being stuck in a matrix organization. Segmentation also makes it simpler to evaluate performance; instead of relying on complicated performance management tools and questionable accounting data to measure and reward success, success is tightly coupled with segment performance. Continued financial success and achievement of strategic goals are the key metrics.

As 80/20 thinkers, the vital few people understand imbalances and think in asymmetric terms. They expect and believe there is a simpler way to achieve results without having to walk down the complex beaten path. They are always looking for shortcuts and prefer to be selective rather than exhaustive. They have a mind-set of making things happen with the least possible effort (but without cutting corners) by focusing only on what they do best. They tend to work less and delegate more while pursuing a limited number of alternatives, rather than going after every available opportunity. They also expect continuous change, so they track their markets very closely and are open to unexpected possibilities.

The best people enjoy working and thriving in lean entrepreneurial environments. They understand that running a BU means that their team is it. There is very little or no corporate safety net. There is no central legal department, for example, or at least not a large one, to help with legal issues that pop up out of the blue. The BU must use outside law firms, if necessary, to help resolve issues. Being a BU leader means being responsible for many areas of a business that you don't normally worry about when you work in a large monolithic corporation. In 80/20 driven BUs, every employee counts. No one can be left behind or remain untrained, not knowing what to do. Everyone is a sales person. Everyone takes care of the customer. This is the ultimate upside down pyramid. Everyone works for the last guy on the production line who is supporting the customer.

The work of the BU general manager can be summarized into six areas:

1. Shaping the work environment and creating an 80/20 mind-set—general managers set high standards of performance and give the example for others to follow. They raise expectations for other managers, set goals, ask critical questions, and get involved in determining the company's values. They develop a distinctive work environment based on 80/20 thinking and business practices.

2. Crafting the UVP and strategic vision—general managers lead the creation and continuous evolution of the UVP and strategy, spearheading innovative thinking in more dimensions than just product invention.

3.  Ensuring that resources are properly focused on the "eighty"—general managers concentrate resources on areas that provide leverage and comparative advantage for the BU in the market. They think like the business owner, focusing on fewer opportunities to get behind and aggressively supporting their people to fully develop these opportunities.

4.  Identifying and developing "eighty" people—general managers act selectively to identify and develop the vital few people and make tough decisions about people in general. They do not try to rationalize poor performance by hoping that experience will help improve weak managers. They lead the performance review and succession process based on both results and behavior.

5.  Building a dynamic organization—general managers find ways to weed complexity out of the organization and become personally involved in solving important problems, regardless of what the organization chart says. They bring managers together to talk about the business, to get input on important projects, and to line up their support.

6.  Running the business to get results—general managers meet commitments and don't miss profit goals every year because of unexpected events. If business drops off sharply, they scale back costs, cut discretionary expenses, and eliminate losers. They don't commit the business to more things than it can handle or to a pace that falls short of its capacity.

The question that always comes up at this point is how you find such people. How do you pick the vital few from the trivial many? But the answer is very simple. Expose everyone in the business to 80/20 thinking and to the UVP of running their own P&L in a focused BU—the vital few will reveal themselves. They will get it right away. It's like attracting "eighty" customers to your portfolio with a UVP. It's also like the "rack the shotgun" story by Perry Marshall that illustrates how to identify new customers that will pay more for your UVP (see chapter 2 in his book).[liv] The vital few are naturally drawn to the idea of autonomy and accountability. At the same time, the trivial many will tend to stay away from your UVP, at least for a while. The majority of the people will support and understand, but they will probably not want to lead the BU until they are convinced of success.

Peter Drucker has written one of his finest articles in Harvard Business Review called "What Makes an Effective Executive," which is very appropriate to quote:

*"An effective executive does not need to be a leader in the sense that the term is now most commonly used. Harry Truman did not have one ounce of charisma, for example, yet he was among the most effective chief executives in US history. Similarly, some of the best business and nonprofit CEOs I've worked with over a 65-year consulting career were not stereotypical leaders. They were all over the map in terms of their personalities, attitudes, values, strengths, and weaknesses. They ranged from extroverted to nearly reclusive, from easygoing to controlling, from generous to parsimonious."*

*What made them all effective is that they followed the same eight practices:*

- *They asked, "What needs to be done?"*
- *They asked, "What is right for the enterprise?"*
- *They developed action plans.*
- *They took responsibility for decisions.*
- *They took responsibility for communicating.*
- *They were focused on opportunities rather than problems.*
- *They ran productive meetings.*
- *They thought and said "we" rather than "I."*

*"The first two practices gave them the knowledge they needed. The next four helped them convert this knowledge into effective action. The last two ensured that the whole organization felt responsible and accountable."*[iv]

These practices speak directly to the heart of the issue related to identifying and empowering BU leaders. They need to possess the intellectual humility to ask what is right for the business and be willing to listen and let the data talk. Critical thinking and data-based analysis are essential. They also need to apply the 80/20 thinking frequently and delegate, allowing vital few people to do what they do best. They should not make decisions or take actions in areas where they are not the best.

There is also an emerging profile of BU leaders that comes from intense economic globalization and also from what is called commoditization of knowledge. I've seen firsthand the impact that these management tsunamis had on industrial and established companies during the past two decades, and they obviously influence the ways we will think about leadership going forward.

## Global Leadership in the Era of Commoditized Knowledge

To become effective and successful these days, leaders need to move beyond embracing frequent change; they need to enjoy it. Changing target market segments, changing BUs, changing companies, and changing countries are common features in the life of a modern executive. Evolution, innovation, and the fractal nature of markets don't know geographical borders. Besides an adventurous spirit coupled with the desire to change, executives need a rich toolbox with different language skills, global networking skills, and a personalized work system that is continuously adapted and enriched after every engagement.

In this global and truly connected economy, there is major and disproportional opportunity for 80/20 thinkers who act and behave as free agents. Contrary to traditional company lovers or company loyalists, the free agent executive sees his or her role in a company as a transformational one, with a mission to be accomplished rather than a job to hold on to. Missions typically last a couple of years but generally not a lifetime.

Free agent leaders combine independence with 80/20 and critical thinking, developing deep self-awareness. They know what they believe in and what makes them different from other executives. This is critical for tolerance development and adaptability in a world full of diversity and idiosyncrasies. James Clawson described in his book the eleven key characteristics of a global business leader: "Overseas experience, deep self-awareness, sensitivity to cultural diversity, humility, lifelong curiosity, cautious honesty, global strategic thinking, patiently impatient, well-spoken, good negotiator, and presence."[lvi] These are all important in a changing world, especially considering that all countries, rich or poor, are rapidly becoming equals when it comes to information access and knowledge base.

But what is different now? What has changed? We are living in a world that has an abundance of many things that were considered scarce just a couple of decades ago, such as access to information and food (at least in the developed world). Obesity, for example, has become a national health problem in most industrialized nations. It's almost impossible not to draw a parallel between food that makes us obese and information that makes us unfocused. But is it possible to become obese and oversaturated with information? I believe so.

A case in point is the obsessive use of social media. It's easy to see how much time and attention is spent on e-mail and social networks nowadays. People have become addicted to information and communication technologies by entirely relying on these means to interact with their networks and to acquire information. In the process, we can spend hours and days focusing on useless or plainly false knowledge that comes along with the nuggets we are mining for. It does not seem like good management of the most precious resource we have—time.

When it comes to business, instead of setting aside 20 percent of the workday for productive and uninterrupted focused thinking, as prescribed by Peter Drucker in The Effective Executive[lvii], more and more managers are averaging their attention span throughout the workday and giving the same or more quality attention to the trivial many as to the vital few. More managers have become so accustomed to relying on commoditized information sources that they almost completely disregard the importance of their own business analytics and critical thinking skills to determine what is best for the business.

Commoditization of knowledge is a trend impacting all knowledge workers and managers. As industry expertise and skills become easily available through the Internet and other means, knowledge loses differentiation and value across the board, becoming a commodity. Knowledge has a shelf life and it continues to shrink. Relying on shelved knowledge to run the business can no longer guarantee a comparative advantage.

GLG Group is a good example of a company tapping into this trend to market open knowledge. GLG is the "world's largest membership network for one-on-one professional learning, comprising more than 400,000 thought leaders and practitioners, including business leaders, scientists, academics, former public sector leaders and the foremost subject matter specialists."[lviii] GLG has more than 1,400 client companies in forty countries in nearly every sector, including the leading professional services firms and financial institutions.

To innovate and grow today, business leaders need to be capable of constantly creating differentiated knowledge, using firsthand data from their markets, applying analytical tools such as the CP matrix, and using 80/20 thinking coupled with critical thinking. The best results will go to those who can continuously apply 80/20 to distinguish sources of information, create differentiated segments and customer knowledge, and develop true UVPs for customers.

Leaders who are fully capable of discriminating their focus and attention to create differentiated knowledge will be able to capitalize the most from this new era. These people navigate through the information overload maze and take time every workday to perform focused thinking, even if only for ninety minutes. They embrace networking and analytics in the era of big data and mine nuggets of precious information using their own mining methodologies and going through their own critical thinking processes.

These attributes are no longer exclusive to pure knowledge industries like software design, for example. They are also a must for conventional businesses, like manufacturers and distributors. Therefore, combining all the aspects above, the most relevant attributes to look for in people to lead BUs in the global and commoditized knowledge era are represented in the leadership tower in figure 47.

**The 80/20 leadership tower:**

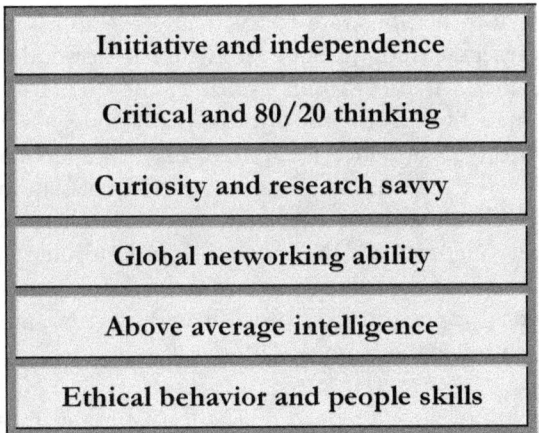

Figure 47.

Ethical behavior and people skills are at the foundation of the leadership tower. Without them, the tower will not stand. Ethical people not only know the difference between right and wrong, but they also strive to set an example of good conduct. They also apply principles of fairness and honesty with coworkers, customers, suppliers, and whomever they come in contact with. The golden rule is the natural law here: they treat others as they would want to be treated themselves. These behaviors are not only fundamental, but it's common knowledge that they are also good for business—they provide employee retention, customer loyalty, improved work environments, and a shield against legal liabilities.

As the 80/20 principle points out, people are not all the same. There is a natural imbalance in the intelligence area, and managers should use this asymmetry in their favor when hiring. However, when it comes to business leadership, there are multiple forms of intelligence to ponder: IQ, emotional, educational, social, creative, analytical, and practical. IQ alone is not a good predictor of intelligence, so managers must consider a combination of traits that best reflect what is needed for the business.

Global networking ability is primarily the skill and ability that leaders have to communicate well with markets, customers, employees, suppliers, and communities at a global level. It's the experience, understanding, and style of developing deeper connections with a variety of people around the world. Most global leaders already have a wealth of connections and relationships that can be leveraged in any new position.

Leaders have to demonstrate curiosity and research savvy—the ability to constantly learn new things in an ever-changing world. At the same time, with the abundance of information available, they need to know how to separate the vital few from the trivial many nuggets of knowledge. Intellectual curiosity is an individual trait that compels these people to proactively look for expansions, reasons, and explanations beyond the obvious. These individuals have a constant appetite to learn what went right and what went wrong, to learn the root cause of a problem, and to educate themselves and others about their markets and the competition. They are at ease with analytical tools and like to do their own data gathering to know the facts. They embrace the truth.

Given the importance of both 80/20 thinking and critical thinking, I have devoted an entire chapter to this subject. The need to develop and identify people who can think in such ways is linked with the ability to lead businesses to innovate and to create comparative advantages in the market. Without asymmetric and differentiated thinking based on firsthand data and analysis, there is less opportunity to create lasting value and a wide economic moat.

At the top of the leadership tower, we have two characteristics—initiative and independence. These identify leaders who like to run their own shows and don't need to be reminded about the importance of profitable growth. However, remember you are not looking for the lone wolf but for the leader of the pack. These are people who want to run a

P&L, even if they have to assume all the small responsibilities associated with running a stand-alone business. You need people with enough entrepreneurial blood in their veins to want to segment the business and create a new BU from scratch. A quote from the author Stephen Covey summarizes these attributes really well: "The key is taking responsibility and initiative, deciding what your life is about and prioritizing your life around the most important things."[lix]

# CONCLUSION

There isn't a single formula to capitalize on the natural laws or to apply the 80/20 methodology. Acquiring or developing tools based on natural principles combined with 80/20 thinking and behavior toward selectiveness and simplicity will drive results. In fact, it is possible to create a custom improvement system based on the four natural principles for any unique situation, and it will probably end up being an effective way to reach new performance levels, if applied with discipline.

There are different menus or levels of adoption of the 80/20 BPI that can be used depending on the level of commitment to 80/20 and the past implementation experience available in the organization. Many companies opt to start small and experiment with the thinking and the analytics before they move on to optimize and fully convert the business to 80/20, which requires a more definite commitment. I've learned this process is not always intuitive; therefore, it helps to start with data analysis. After a few implementations, companies usually acquire the confidence to launch a more complete plan, encompassing analytics, optimization, and full conversion all at once. All of these plans respect the natural sequence of steps or implementation cycle.

The most basic level or the first stage is the thinking stage, and it only requires the 80/20 mind-set to be present while planning and developing strategy. The mere fact that leaders are making an effort to become selective and to focus on a vital few initiatives can start the transformation. Signs that 80/20 thinking is present are that leaders are managing the company as a portfolio of businesses and that their strategies and planning are focused on a vital few initiatives.

The second stage is the analytics stage, which makes pervasive use of data and analysis. It requires a small commitment of resources to develop the CP matrix and the quad analysis. Coupled with the 80/20 thinking, managers will create an optimization plan for customers and products, setting goals for sales and contribution margins. A complexity analysis is done using transaction data. The evidence that a business has reached this stage includes the following:

- CP matrix and quad analysis executed
- Planning and optimization ideas developed
- Attention paid to sweet spots
- Complexity matrix executed

The third stage is optimization (or adjustment). The business has the mind-set, the analytics, and the plan to start making changes to the portfolio and to focus more intensely on customer segments, without going into full-blown segmentation or revamping its manufacturing footprint. Companies here use analytics on a routine basis in order to impact pricing, commercial policies, and other strategies covered in this book. They simplify their product portfolios using PLS and improve business processes with BPS in order to have different policies for "eighty" and "twenty" customers and products. They also start using direct costing and contribution margins analytically, without completely changing their accounting systems, creating new productivity and complexity metrics. Innovation workshops and high scrutiny for new part numbers entering the system are also present. We find evidence of the following activities:

- Use of 80/20 analytics on a routine basis
- Use of filters and sales incentives to prevent unwanted business exist
- Use of different policies for key and nonkey customers and products
- Use of direct costing and contribution margins analytically
- Application of productivity and complexity metrics
- Selling of "twenty" products only at the request of "eighty" customers (most of the time)
- Focus on innovation for key customers and markets
- Establishment of contribution margin targets

Conversion is the more advanced or higher stage when the company goes into full implementation mode, making the commitment to physically separate the "eighty" from the "twenty," utilizing in-lines for high-volume products, and potentially outsourcing a large number of low-volume parts. Companies adopt direct cost method and full utilization of 80/20 metrics.

There are robust processes for systematic innovation in place and for ensuring that new part numbers only enter the system after passing through the acid test. We normally see the following activities at this stage:

- Use of 80/20 analytics beyond the CP matrix (e.g., in purchasing)
- Repricing and purging of all unwanted business
- Creation of in-lines for "eighty" products
- Physical separation of "eighty" and "twenty" products
- Outsourcing of low-volume products
- Integration of direct costing across the organization
- Utilization of complexity metrics
- Innovation beyond product invention

Regardless of the menu adopted, the critical requirement is that leaders fully embrace and commit to the mind-set and the thinking before starting. Without the commitment to selectiveness in strategy definition and planning, there is little chance of success. The vital few inputs (the choices) must be clear, visible, and separated from the trivial many inputs (the nonchoices) to provide clear direction and avoid complexity. Nonchoices are potential initiatives or strategic choices that have been consciously de-selected from the strategic plan, because they are not part of the vital few inputs.

Managers need to be critical to ensure they have only chosen initiatives that can cause favorable imbalances toward their goals. At the same time, they must single out and isolate the nonchoices or initiatives that will not be pursued. This exercise to find asymmetry can be done with 80/20 thinking alone, but it is most productive when performed with data analysis that shows where the imbalances lie. An excessive number of priorities and metrics is a clear sign that the mind-set and the thinking have not taken hold yet. In this case, less is clearly more.

Finally, this is an evergreen process, a continuum that is always regenerating and dividing, like a healthy cell, propelled by the four natural laws. It really changes the business for better and relatively quickly, compared to other methodologies. It leads to transformational growth and the creation of a new business model and singularity for the company. It creates a wide and deep economic moat.

RECCOMENDED READING AND ENDNOTES

## ADDITIONAL INFORMATION SOURCES - BOOKS

| TITLE | | | |
|---|---|---|---|
| AUTHOR | PUBLISHER | EDITION | DATE |
| Business Model Generation: A Handbook for Visionaries, Game Changers, and Challengers | | | |
| Alexander Osterwalder and Yves Pigneur | John Wiley and Sons | 1 | 7/13/2010 |
| Innovation Training (ASTD Trainer's Workshop) | | | |
| Ruth Ann Hattori and Joyce Wycoff | ASTD Press | n/a | 6/1/2004 |
| Managing Complexity in Global Organizations | | | |
| Ulrich Steger, Wolfgang Amann and Martha Maznevski | Wiley | 1 | 5/7/2007 |
| The Innovator's Dilemma: The Revolutionary Book That Will Change the Way You Do Business | | | |
| Clayton M. Christensen | HarperBusiness | Reprint edition | 10/4/2011 |
| The Innovator's Solution: Creating and Sustaining Successful Growth | | | |
| Clayton M. Christensen and Michael E. Raynor | Harvard Business Review Press | 1 | 10/22/2013 |
| The Innovator's Toolkit: 50+ Techniques for Predictable and Sustainable Organic Growth | | | |
| David Silverstein, Philip Samuel and Neil DeCarlo | Wiley | 1 | 10/27/2008 |
| Six Thinking Hats | | | |
| Edward de Bono | Back Bay Books | 2 | 8/18/1999 |
| Trizics: Teach yourself TRIZ, how to invent, innovate and solve "impossible" technical problems systematically | | | |

| AUTHOR | PUBLISHER | EDITION | DATE |
|---|---|---|---|
| | | TITLE | |
| Gordon Cameron | CreateSpace Independent Publishing Platform | | 11/9/2010 |
| Level Three Leadership: Getting Below the Surface | | | |
| James G. Clawson | Prentice Hall | 5 | 1/14/2011 |
| The Laws of Simplicity (Simplicity: Design, Technology, Business, Life) | | | |
| John Maeda | The MIT Press | First full edition | 8/21/2006 |
| Systematic Innovation: An Introduction to TRIZ (Theory of Inventive Problem Solving) | | | |
| John Terninko, Alla Zusman and Boris Zlotin | CRC Press | 1 | 4/15/1998 |
| Ten Types of Innovation: The Discipline of Building Breakthroughs | | | |
| Larry Keeley and Helen Walters | Wiley | 1 | 7/15/2013 |
| 80/20 Sales and Marketing: The Definite Guide to Working Less and Making More | | | |
| Perry Marshall | Entrepreneur Press | n/a | 7/22/2013 |
| The Effective Executive: The Definitive Guide to Getting the Right Things Done | | | |
| Peter F. Drucker | HaperBusiness | Revised | 1/2/2006 |
| The Practice of Management | | | |
| Peter F. Drucker | HarperBusiness | Reissue edition | 10/3/2006 |
| What Makes an Effective Executive | | | |

| AUTHOR | PUBLISHER | EDITION | DATE |
|--------|-----------|---------|------|
| Peter F. Drucker | Harvard Business Review Press | 1 | 1/3/2011 |

The 80/20 Principle: The Secret to Achieving More with Less

| AUTHOR | PUBLISHER | EDITION | DATE |
|--------|-----------|---------|------|
| Richard Koch | Crown Business | Reprint | 10/19/1999 |

The Natural Laws of Business: How to Harness the Power of Evolution, Physics, and Economics to Achieve Business Success

| AUTHOR | PUBLISHER | EDITION | DATE |
|--------|-----------|---------|------|
| Richard Koch | Crown Business | 1 | 8/14/2001 |

The Balanced Scorecard: Translating Strategy into Action

| AUTHOR | PUBLISHER | EDITION | DATE |
|--------|-----------|---------|------|
| Robert S. Kaplan and David P. Norton | Harvard Business Review Press | 1 | 9/1/1996 |

Strategy Maps: Converting Intangible Assets into Tangible Outcomes

| AUTHOR | PUBLISHER | EDITION | DATE |
|--------|-----------|---------|------|
| Robert S. Kaplan and David P. Norton | Harvard Business Review Press | 1 | 2/2/2004 |

Grow from Within: Mastering Corporate Entrepreneurship and Innovation

| AUTHOR | PUBLISHER | EDITION | DATE |
|--------|-----------|---------|------|
| Robert Wolcott and Michael Lippitz | McGraw-Hill Education | 1 | 10/13/2009 |

Blur: The Speed of Change in the Connected Economy

| AUTHOR | PUBLISHER | EDITION | DATE |
|--------|-----------|---------|------|
| Stan Davis and Christopher Meyer | Grand Central Publishing | 1 | 4/1/1999 |

Seven Habits of Highly Effective People

| AUTHOR | PUBLISHER | EDITION | DATE |
|--------|-----------|---------|------|
| Stephen Covey | Simon Schuster Ltd UK | Illustrated edition | 6/12/1905 |

# ADDITIONAL INFORMATION SOURCES – WEBSITES

| WEBSITE | SPONSOR | LAST ACCESSED |
|---|---|---|
| URL | | |
| www.deming.org | | |
| Deming Institute | The W. Edwards Deming Institute | Jun., 2015 |
| www.doblin.com | | |
| Doblin | Deloitte Touche Tohmatsu Limited | Sep., 2015 |
| www.fractalfoundation.org | | |
| Fractal Foundation | Fractal Foundation | Jun., 2015 |
| www.henrygeorgefoundation.gov | | |
| Henry George Foundation | Henry George Foundation | Sep., 2015 |
| http://hucosystems.com/articles/The_80_20_Principle_2.htm | | |
| Hubert Crowell (What is 80/20) | Hubert Crowell | Sep., 2015 |
| www.mindtools.com | | |
| MindTools | Mind Tools Ltd. | Oct., 2015 |
| www.the8020principle.com | | |
| The 80/20 Principle.com | Richard Koch | Oct., 2015 |
| www.triz40.com | | |
| TRIZ40 | SolidCreativity | Oct., 2015 |

---

[i] Vilfredo Federico Damaso Pareto (born Wilfried Fritz Pareto) was an Italian engineer, sociologist, economist, political scientist, and philosopher. He lived from July 15, 1848–August 19, 1923.

[ii] Joseph Moses Juran (Dec 24, 1904–Feb 28, 2008) was a Romanian-born American engineer and management consultant.

[iii] The Practice of Management by Peter F. Drucker – HarperBusiness – Reissue edition (10/3/2006).

[iv] ITW: forging the tools for excellence / Kris Frieswick. -1st edition - Fenwick Publishing Group, Inc. – page 108 (2012).

[v] Henry George (September 2, 1839–October 29, 1897).

[vi] Excerpt from David Triggs – Chairman, Henry George Foundation – www.henrygeorgefoundation.gov - Retrieved on July/2009.

[vii] Excerpt from David Triggs – Chairman, Henry George Foundation -– www.henrygeorgefoundation.gov. - Retrieved on July/2009.

[viii] Adam Smith, The Wealth of Nations (1776) – Bantam Classics, Reprint Edition (3/4/2003).

[ix] Excerpt from GSI (Global Subsidies Initiative) International Environment website - http://www.iisd.org - Retrieved in October/2015.

[x] Joseph Moses Juran (December 24, 1904–February 28, 2008) was a Romanian-born American management consultant and engineer. Vilfredo Federico Damaso Pareto (born Wilfried Fritz Pareto) was an Italian engineer, sociologist, economist, political scientist, and philosopher. He lived from July 15, 1848–August 19, 1923.

[xi] Peter Drucker, The Effective Executive, HarperBusiness; Revised edition (January 3, 2006).

[xii] John Maeda, *The Laws of Simplicity* (Simplicity: Design, Technology, Business, Life), The MIT Press; First Thus edition (August 21, 2006).

xiii Henry David Thoreau Citation – GoodReads – https://www.goodreads.com - Retrieved October, 2015.

xiv Definition from Fractal Foundation (www.fractalfoundation.org) - Retrieved on October 2015.

xv YourDictionary definition and usage example. http://www.yourdictionary.com/evolution - Retrieved on October, 2015.

xvi Jillian D'Onfro, *Business Insider Magazine* (July 12, 2015).

xvii Netflix: The Turnaround Story of 2012 - www.forbes.com - Retrieved in January 2013.

xviii Sir Richard Charles Nicholas Branson, Kt (born 18 July 1950) is an English businessman and investor. He is best known as the founder of Virgin Group, which comprises more than 400 companies.

xix Richard Branson's Top 10 Tips for Succeeding at Business - www.entrepreneur.com - Retrieved in September, 2015.

xx The W. Edwards Deming Institute www.deming.or - Retrieved on June, 2015.

xxi Chris Gallant, "What is an economic moat?" – www.*investopedia.com* - *Retrieved in September*, 2015.

xxii Hubert Crowell – Simple is Beautiful  (The cost of complexity) - http://hucosystems.com/articles/The_80_20_Principle_6.htm - Retrieved on October, 2015.

xxiii Hubert Crowell – Simple is Beautiful (Go for the most simple 20 percent)

- http://hucosystems.com/articles/The_80_20_Principle_6.htm - Retrieved on October, 2015.

xxiv Ulrich Steger, Wolfgang Amann and Martha Maznevski - Managing Complexity in Global Organizations (IMD Executive Development

Series) - Wiley; 1st. edition (May 7, 2007).

xxv H. Thomas Johnson and Anders Broms, Association for Manufacturing Excellence (AME) Magazine - "The Spirit in the Walls: A Pattern for High Performance at Scania," (May/June 1995).

xxvi "ITW Business Philosophies" E-Learning Program - http://itwelearning.com/pdf_files/ITW%20Business%20Philosophies_Course%20Summaries.pdf - Retrieved on 7/5/14.

xxvii CIMA – Activity Based Costing http://www.cimaglobal.com/Documents/ImportedDocuments/cid_tg_activity_based_costing_nov08.pdf.pdf - Retrieve in October, 2015.

xxviii Warren E. Buffett, 1979 letter to Berkshire Hathaway investors (published March 3, 1980), http://www.berkshirehathaway.com/letters/1979.html - Retrieved on October, 2015.

xxix Citation from Phillip Kotler and Kevin Keller - Marketing Management - Prentice Hall; 14 edition (February 18, 2011).

xxx Paul Green and Donald Tull, Research for Marketing Decisions - Prentice-Hall international series in management - Longman Higher Education; 4th edition (March 1978).

xxxi Alexander Osterwalder and Yves Pigneur, Business Model Generation: A Handbook for Visionaries, Game Changers, and Challengers - John Wiley and Sons; 1st edition (July 13, 2010).

xxxii Investopedia – Definition of "Zero-Based Budgeting – ZBB, http://www.investopedia.com/terms/z/zbb.asp, Retrieved on October 2015.

xxxiii Perry Marshall, 80/20 Sales and Marketing: The Definitive Guide to Working Less and Making More, Entrepreneur Press (2013).

xxxiv Chris Disher, Matthew Egol and Leslie Moeller – Smart Customization: Profitable Growth Through Tailored Business Streams – Booz Allen Hamilton, 2003.

xxxv Article by Matt Linderman (wrote on March 27 2007) – Signal v. Noise website -https://signalvnoise.com/posts/333-warren-buffett-on-castles-and-moats - Retrieved in September 2015.

xxxvi Clayton Christensen, The Innovator's Dilemma (Harvard Business Review Press, Reprint edition, October 4 2011).

xxxvii Clayton Christensen and Michael Raynor, The Innovator's Solution (Harvard Business School Press; 1 edition (September2003).

xxxviii Karan Girotra and Serguei Netessine, "Four Paths to Business Model Innovation," Harvard Business Review (July–August 2014 issue).

xxxix Developed in the 80s by Dr Noriaki Kano, professor emeritus of the Tokyo University of Science.

xl Technique originally developed by Sakichi Toyoda and adopted by Taiichi Ohno, the architect of the Toyota Production System (TPS).

xli Ruth Ann Hattori and Joyce Wycoff - Innovation Training (ASTD Trainer's Workshop) - ASTD (January 10, 2006).

xlii Alex F. Osborn – Applied Imagination – Scribner, June 1979.

xliii Edward de Bono – Six Thinking Hats – Back Bay Books; 2 edition (August 18, 1999).

xliv Information from TRIZ40 by SolidCreativity – http://www.triz40.com - Retrieved in September 2015.

xlv Patents databases – one example: www.triz40.com/patents.php.

xlvi "TRIZ Matrix," the TRIZ40 website, http://www.triz40.com/aff_Matrix_TRIZ.php

xlvii "The 40 TRIZ Principles," the TRIZ40 website, http://www.triz40.com/aff_Principles_TRIZ.php

xlviii MindTools - Management Training and Leadership Training, Online – www.mindtools.com - Retrieved on October, 2015.

[xlix] Doblin – Member of Deloitte Touche Tohmatsu Limited – www.doblin.com - Retrieved on September 2015.

[l] Robert Wolcott on Innovation as a Business Design Challenge – MSI (Marketing Science Institute) - http://www.msi.org/articles/think-about-innovation-as-a-business-design-challenge/ - Retrieved on September 2015.

[li] Examples from Kairos Management – Examples based on Doblin's Ten Types of Innovation – www.kairosmanagement.com - Retrieved in June 2015.

[lii] Doblin – Member of Deloitte Touche Tohmatsu Limited – www.doblin.com - Retrieved on September 2015

[liii] Larry Keeley, Helen Walters, Ryan Pikkel, and Brian Quinn, Ten Types of Innovation: The Discipline of Building Breakthroughs, Wiley; 1 edition (July 15, 2013).

[liv] Perry Marshall, 80/20 Sales and Marketing: The Definitive Guide to Working Less and Making More – Chapter 2 – Entrepreneur Press, 2013.

[lv] Peter F. Drucker, "What Makes an Effective Executive," *Harvard Business Review* (June 2004), page 1.

[lvi] Level Three Leadership: Getting Below the Surface – James G. Clawson – Prentice Hall; 5 edition (1/14/2011).

[lvii] The Effective Executive: The Definitive Guide to Getting the Right Things Done (HarperBusiness Essentials) – Peter F. Drucker – HarperBusiness; Revised edition (1/3/2006).

[lviii] Gerson Lehrman Group, Inc. (GLG) – Company website – www.glggroup.com - Retrieved in September 2015.

[lix] Seven Habits of Highly Effective People – Stephen Covey – Simon Schuster Ltd UK – Illustrated edition (1990).

# ABOUT THE AUTHOR

Pedro N Ferro is an accomplished executive with 25 years of experience managing manufacturing and technology businesses. He has degrees in mechanical and industrial engineering, having spent most of his professional life working outside of his native Brazil. He is currently the CEO of Fras-Le, a global friction materials company. Pedro has led many 80/20 implementations throughout his career in different companies. He is married with two daughters, and is a resident of Charlotte, North Carolina. Pedro is and avid motorcyclist and enjoys teaching 80/20.
Pedro can be reached at pnferro@gmail.com.